THE AUTHOR'S COMPANION

A WORKBOOK FOR 'WRITE IT. PUBLISH IT. SELL IT.'

M.L. RUSCSAK

Copyright © 2024 Trient Press

All rights reserved. No portion of this publication may be reproduced, distributed, or transmitted in any form or by any means, including photocopying, recording, or other electronic or mechanical methods, without the prior written permission of the publisher. This restriction excludes brief quotations utilized in critical reviews and certain other noncommercial usages as permitted by copyright law. For permission inquiries, direct correspondence to the publisher, marked "Attention: Permissions Coordinator," at the following address:
Trient Press
3375 S Rainbow Blvd
#81710, SMB 13135
Las Vegas, NV 89180

Criminal copyright infringement, including instances without financial gain, is subject to investigation by the FBI and incurs penalties of up to five years in federal imprisonment and a fine of $250,000.
Excepting the original narrative material authored by M.L. Ruscsak, all songs, song titles, and lyrics cited within The Author's Companion: A Workbook for 'Write It. Publish It. Sell It.'
remain the exclusive property of their respective artists, songwriters, and copyright holders.
Ordering Information:
For quantity sales, Trient Press offers special discounts to corporations, associations, and other organizations. For detailed information, contact the publisher at the address provided above.
For orders by U.S. trade bookstores and wholesalers, please reach out to Trient Press at
Tel: (775) 996-3844, or visit www.trientpress.com.
Printed in the United States of America
Publisher's Cataloging-in-Publication Data
Ruscsak, M.L.
The Author's Companion: A Workbook for 'Write It. Publish It. Sell It.'

Hardcover: **979-8-88990-205-8**

Paperback: ISBN **979-8-88990-206-5**

E-Book: **979-8-88990-207-2**

Welcome to *The Author's Companion: A Workbook for 'Write It. Publish It. Sell It.'* This workbook is designed to accompany you on your journey through the comprehensive class series that explores the art and science of writing, publishing, and selling your book. Whether you are an aspiring author taking your first steps into the literary world or a seasoned writer looking to refine your skills, this workbook is your trusted guide.

Since publishing my first book in 2016, I have been part of numerous author groups and communities. Over the years, I've noticed that new authors and those contemplating publishing their work often ask the same questions and face similar challenges. It's clear that the path to becoming a successful author is filled with uncertainties, decisions, and a steep learning curve. My hope with this workbook is to provide a clear, structured, and supportive resource that addresses these common concerns and helps you navigate your author journey with confidence and clarity.

Each section of this workbook corresponds to the topics covered in the 'Write It. Publish It. Sell It.' class series. You will find practical exercises, reflective questions, and valuable resources designed to deepen your understanding and enhance your skills. From mastering the writing process to exploring the various publishing options, and from crafting a compelling query letter to building and engaging your audience, this workbook is here to support you every step of the way.

I believe that education and collaboration are the keys to success. By sharing our knowledge and experiences, we can rise together, not as competitors but as colleagues, friends, and most importantly, as a community. My goal with this workbook is to help you avoid the pitfalls that many of us encountered and to guide you towards achieving your publishing dreams.

As you work through the exercises and reflections in this companion, remember that your voice is unique and your story is worth telling. Embrace your journey with passion and persistence. Let this workbook be your companion, offering you the tools, insights, and encouragement you need to write, publish, and sell your book.

Thank you for allowing me to be a part of your author journey.
Together, let's make your dream of becoming a published author a reality.

Your voice as a writer is like a fingerprint—entirely unique to you. It encompasses your style, tone, and perspective, distinguishing your work from that of others. But how do you find this voice, and how do you hone it to perfection? In this section, we will explore techniques to help you discover and develop your unique writing style, ensuring that your voice resonates authentically with your readers.

Exercises for Discovering and Honing Your Unique Writing Style

1. Embrace Your Authentic Self

Exercise: Personal Reflection Writing

- **Task:** Write a short essay about a personal experience that has deeply impacted you. Focus on expressing your emotions and thoughts authentically, without worrying about structure or style.
- **Goal:** To connect with your true self and let your natural voice emerge in your writing.

Example:

Personal Reflection Writing: A Deeply Impacting Experience

The Summer of Change

The summer after I completed a college program for pre-med during my sophomore year of high school was a pivotal time in my life. I was sixteen, filled with dreams of becoming a doctor, when my grandfather fell seriously ill. The diagnosis was severe, and the doctors recommended immediate surgery on his kidney.

The day of his surgery is etched in my memory. The hospital waiting room felt sterile and lifeless, a stark contrast to the vibrant energy my grandfather always exuded. The antiseptic smell was overwhelming, mingling with the faint aroma of stale coffee. As I sat there, surrounded by strangers lost in their own worries, an overwhelming sense of foreboding washed over me. Even at that young age, I could see the writing on the wall—my grandfather might not be coming home.

He had always been a pillar of strength in our family, a man of action rather than words. His hands, worn and calloused from years of hard work, were a testament to a life lived with integrity and perseverance. He taught me the value of hard work through lessons in welding and the use of power tools, skills that require precision and patience. He introduced me to the thrill of flea markets, where we would hunt for hidden treasures and haggle with vendors, teaching me the art of negotiation and the joy of discovery.

More than anything, my grandfather was my guide on the path to becoming a reverend. He nurtured my love for history and people-watching, encouraging me to understand the stories behind every face and the events that shaped our world. His teachings were more than just lessons; they were experiences that molded my character and broadened my horizons.

As I waited for news, these memories flooded my mind, each one a precious moment shared with a man who had shaped my life in so many ways. The wait felt interminable, each second stretching into an eternity. I tried to distract myself with a book, but the words seemed to blur and dance on the page, refusing to provide any comfort. My mind was a whirlwind of thoughts, fears, and hopes, each one competing for attention. I knew that the surgery was risky, and although the doctors were skilled, there was an unspoken understanding that the outcome was uncertain.

Finally, the surgeon came out, his expression grave yet professional. My heart pounded in my chest as he spoke, explaining that the surgery had been complicated. They had managed to remove the tumor, but my grandfather's condition was precarious. Relief mingled with a deep-seated fear; the battle was far from over, and the road to recovery would be long and fraught with challenges.

In the days that followed, I spent every possible moment by my grandfather's bedside. His once robust frame was now frail and vulnerable, a stark reminder of the fragility of life. I held his hand, the same hand that had guided me through so many lessons, and talked to him about everything and nothing. His strength, though diminished, was still there, evident in the way he squeezed my hand, offering silent reassurance.

This experience profoundly changed me. It stripped away the veneer of youthful invincibility and exposed the raw, unfiltered reality of life and death. I discovered a resilience within myself that I hadn't known existed. I found a deeper sense of empathy, not just for my grandfather, but for everyone who faces such profound challenges. Most importantly, I began to understand the importance of authenticity in my own voice, shaped by the trials and triumphs of this journey.

Writing about this experience feels like opening a window to my soul, allowing the light of truth to illuminate the darkest corners. It is a reminder that our most significant moments of growth often arise from the crucible of adversity. In sharing this story, I hope to honor my grandfather's legacy and inspire others to embrace their struggles with courage and grace.

This is my voice—honest, reflective, and deeply human. It is the voice of someone who has walked through the fire and emerged stronger, with a renewed appreciation for the beauty and fragility of life.

_____
_____
_____
_____
_____
_____

2. Experiment with Different Styles and Genres

Exercise: Genre Exploration

- **Task:** Write three short pieces in different genres (e.g., a fictional short story, a personal essay, and a poem). Reflect on which genre felt most comfortable and enjoyable to write.
- **Goal:** To explore various writing styles and identify which ones resonate with you.

Example:

1. Fictional Short Story

Title: The Secret Garden

Elena had always been drawn to the old mansion at the end of Maple Street. It stood there, shrouded in mystery, with ivy crawling up its weathered walls and broken windows that seemed to watch her every move. On her thirteenth birthday, curiosity got the best of her. She slipped through the rusty gates and ventured into the overgrown garden.

There, hidden beneath a canopy of tangled vines, she found an ancient stone door. Her heart raced as she pushed it open, revealing a hidden garden unlike any she had ever seen. Flowers of every color bloomed in wild abandon, and a gentle breeze carried the scent of jasmine and roses. In the center of the garden stood a majestic oak tree, its branches stretching towards the sky like welcoming arms.

Elena felt a strange sense of belonging. As she explored further, she discovered a small, weathered book hidden among the roots of the oak tree. It was filled with stories of the garden's magical past and the secrets it held. From that day on, the garden became her sanctuary, a place where she could escape the mundane and lose herself in the wonders of her imagination.

2. Personal Essay

Title: The Lessons of the Flea Market

Every Sunday morning, my grandfather and I would head to the local flea market. It was a tradition that began when I was ten and continued through my teenage years. The flea market was a bustling maze of stalls, each one brimming with eclectic treasures and hidden gems.

My grandfather had a keen eye for value. He would pick up an old, tarnished item and see its potential, often teaching me about its history and significance. One summer, he taught me how to haggle. At first, I was hesitant, but with his guidance, I learned the art of negotiation. It wasn't just about getting a good deal; it was about understanding the worth of things and standing firm in that knowledge.

These trips were more than just a weekend activity. They were lessons in patience, resilience, and the joy of discovery. They taught me to look beyond the surface, to see the beauty in the imperfect and the value in the forgotten. My grandfather's wisdom, imparted during those flea market adventures, has stayed with me throughout my life, shaping the way I view the world and my place in it.

3. Poem

Title: Echoes of Yesterday

In the garden of memories, Where time's whispers softly sway, Lies a tale of yesteryears, In a place where shadows play.

Beneath the ancient oak's embrace, Secrets linger in the breeze, Whispers of a forgotten past, Carried on the autumn leaves.

The scent of jasmine fills the air, A fragrant kiss from days gone by, Each petal tells a story sweet, Of laughter, love, and lullabies.

Among the roots, a hidden book, Worn pages etched with dreams and tears, A chronicle of hearts once full, Now echoing through the years.

In this garden, time stands still, A sanctuary for the soul, Where echoes of the past remain, And hearts can once again be whole.

Reflection

Writing the fictional short story felt like embarking on an adventure, allowing my imagination to roam freely and create a world of wonder and mystery. The personal essay was a comforting experience, filled with nostalgia and warmth as I recounted cherished memories with my grandfather. The poem, on the other hand, was a deeply introspective journey, weaving emotions and reflections into a tapestry of words.

Among these genres, the personal essay felt most comfortable and enjoyable to write. It allowed me to connect with my past in a meaningful way and express my thoughts and feelings authentically. However, the fictional short story offered a sense of creative freedom that was equally exhilarating, while the poem provided a unique challenge in condensing emotions into a lyrical form.

Each genre offered a different avenue for expression, helping me to explore various facets of my writing voice and discover the styles that resonate most deeply with me.

3. Read Widely and Analytically

Exercise: Analytical Reading Journal

- **Task:** Select excerpts from three different authors you admire. Analyze their writing styles by noting their use of language, sentence structure, tone, and pacing. Write a reflective journal entry on what you learned from each author and how you might incorporate these elements into your own writing.
- **Goal:** To gain insights from different voices and apply those techniques to your own writing.

Analytical Reading Journal: Learning from the Masters

Task: Select excerpts from three different authors you admire. Analyze their writing styles by noting their use of language, sentence structure, tone, and pacing. Write a reflective journal entry on what you learned from each author and how you might incorporate these elements into your own writing.

Excerpt 1: Virginia Woolf

From "To the Lighthouse"

"The sea was indistinguishable from the sky, except that the sea was slightly creased as if a cloth had wrinkles in it; gently the waves slipped into the uttermost rim of the horizon and disappeared."

Analysis:

- **Language:** Woolf uses poetic and descriptive language, creating vivid imagery that blurs the line between reality and perception.
- **Sentence Structure:** Her sentences are often long and flowing, mirroring the continuous movement of the waves she describes.

- **Tone:** The tone is serene and contemplative, evoking a sense of timelessness.
- **Pacing:** The pacing is slow and deliberate, allowing the reader to fully immerse in the moment.

Reflection: Woolf's ability to paint a scene with her words is remarkable. Her descriptive language and fluid sentence structure create a dreamlike quality that draws readers in. I admire how she uses tone and pacing to evoke specific emotions. In my own writing, I aim to incorporate more descriptive language and carefully consider how tone and pacing can enhance the reader's experience, particularly in reflective or introspective passages.

Excerpt 2: Gabriel García Márquez

From "One Hundred Years of Solitude"

"Many years later, as he faced the firing squad, Colonel Aureliano Buendía was to remember that distant afternoon when his father took him to discover ice."

Analysis:

- **Language:** García Márquez uses evocative and symbolic language that hints at the magical realism of his narrative.
- **Sentence Structure:** The sentence is long but structured in a way that seamlessly combines past and future events.
- **Tone:** The tone is mysterious and foreboding, setting the stage for the story's unfolding drama.
- **Pacing:** The pacing is swift, propelling the reader immediately into the narrative while also providing a glimpse of future events.

Reflection: García Márquez's writing style captivates me with its blend of magical realism and profound symbolism. His ability to intertwine different timelines in a single sentence adds depth to the narrative. I want to experiment with similar techniques in my writing, using symbolic language and non-linear storytelling to create a richer, more layered narrative.

Excerpt 3: Ernest Hemingway

From "The Old Man and the Sea"

"He was an old man who fished alone in a skiff in the Gulf Stream and he had gone eighty-four days now without taking a fish."

Analysis:

- **Language:** Hemingway's language is simple and direct, yet powerfully evocative.
- **Sentence Structure:** His sentences are short and to the point, reflecting his minimalist style.
- **Tone:** The tone is straightforward and unembellished, conveying the stark reality of the old man's situation.
- **Pacing:** The pacing is measured, allowing the reader to absorb the gravity of the old man's plight.

Reflection: Hemingway's minimalist style is a testament to the power of simplicity. His ability to convey profound themes with straightforward language and concise sentences is inspiring. I aim to incorporate this minimalist approach in my own writing, focusing on clarity and precision to evoke strong emotions without unnecessary embellishment.

Reflective Journal Entry

Reading these excerpts has provided me with valuable insights into different writing styles and techniques. Virginia Woolf's descriptive and poetic language shows the power of creating vivid imagery and setting a reflective tone. Gabriel García Márquez's use of magical realism and non-linear storytelling demonstrates how to weave complexity into a narrative, making it more engaging and profound. Ernest Hemingway's minimalist approach highlights the effectiveness of simplicity and directness in conveying deep emotions and themes.

Incorporating these elements into my writing, I plan to:

- **Use more descriptive and poetic language** in scenes that require a reflective or introspective tone, much like Woolf does.
- **Experiment with symbolic language and non-linear storytelling** to add depth and intrigue to my narratives, inspired by García Márquez.
- **Embrace simplicity and precision** in my language, ensuring that each word carries weight and contributes to the overall impact of the story, following Hemingway's example.

By blending these techniques, I hope to develop a versatile writing style that resonates with you on multiple levels, creating rich, immersive experiences that are both thought-provoking and emotionally compelling.

4. Write Regularly and Reflect

Exercise: Daily Writing Practice

- **Task:** Set aside 15-30 minutes daily to write about any topic of your choice. At the end of each week, review your entries and note any recurring themes, tones, or styles.
- **Goal:** To develop a consistent writing habit and observe the natural evolution of your voice.

Example:

Daily Writing Practice: Fantasy Realm from " The Fallen of Lite and Darke" rewrite – Chapter 2: Starlis

Task: Set aside 15-30 minutes daily to write about any topic of your choice. At the end of each week, review your entries and note any recurring themes, tones, or styles.

Goal: To develop a consistent writing habit and observe the natural evolution of your voice.

Day 1: Entering the Throne Room

Starlis carried herself with an air of unyielding dignity as she entered the opulent throne room. Her gaze, unwavering and resolute, remained fixed on the queen, her mother, who sat enshrined upon her throne. Approaching the foot of the dais, Starlis confronted her mother's penetrating glare, noting her father standing just a shade behind the throne. His midnight black hair was as disheveled as ever, a stark contrast to the queen's meticulous aura, yet akin in the darkness that seemed to envelop him.

"Mother?" Starlis' voice cut through the thick air, a mix of formality and suppressed emotion.

Day 2: The Sharp Retort

"Shouldn't you be immersed in your studies? You have much to learn before you are deemed fit to ascend to this throne," came her mother's response, sharp as shattered glass, cutting through any pretense of maternal warmth.

Starlis internalized the sting of her mother's words, vowing to herself that she would one day be rid of that piercing, glass-like tone. She studied her mother's features intently, memorizing every detail—the unnaturally pale skin devoid of any luminescent shimmers, the hollowed silver eyes with mere flecks of gold, and the sheer dress that left little to the imagination. A dress that symbolized the transparency of her mother's disdain.

Day 3: The Announcement

Starlis felt a surge of loathing, deeper than any she had known before. Primitiva had always shouldered the burden of their collective resentment, but now, in her absence, the weight fell solely on Starlis' shoulders.

"Primitiva is gone," she announced, her voice carrying a mixture of accusation and concealed grief.

Queen Despina's reaction to Starlis's news was one of uncharacteristic horror. "Gone? What do you mean she's gone?" Her voice trembled with an emotion rarely displayed.

Day 4: Explaining the Disappearance

Starlis, surprised by this display of distress from her usually stoic mother, raised her hands in a gesture of pacification. It was a rarity in Lunaista, or any of the Star Cities for that matter, to witness such turmoil. "She's just vanished," Starlis explained, maintaining a calm and respectful tone despite the storm of emotions inside her. "I believe she chose the Void. Her disdain for the catacombs and her refusal to marry any prince from the

Star Cities were well known. You're aware she always rebelled against the rules, Mother. And the idea of being a traditional mother was never in her plans."

Day 5: The Queen's Despair

Despina sank back into her crystal throne, a look of despair clouding her features. "Do you grasp the gravity of her actions? She's doomed our family... and your future."

Starlis had always perceived her mother as a heartless ruler, so this semblance of concern seemed almost theatrical. "Mother, the laws aren't as rigid as we've believed. The decree states that a tribute from the royal lineage must be offered before a new ruler ascends. It doesn't specify which family member."

Day 6: The Father's Role

"Your father is the only other option!" Despina exclaimed, her voice escalating into a scream.

Starlis, unable to mask her frustration, rolled her eyes. Her mother's demeanor was more akin to a petulant child than a sovereign. "If you continue to uphold this archaic tradition, then you are as responsible for what follows as Primitiva," she retorted. Turning her back on Despina, she added, "I must now prepare for my ascension. It's best not to dwell on this... We wouldn't want Primitiva's alleged dishonor to overshadow the coronation."

Day 7: The Walk Away

As she walked away, Starlis knew that the gossip and whispers that would inevitably follow held little significance for her. Her focus was elsewhere, on the daunting path that lay ahead.

Weekly Reflection

Reviewing my entries this week, several recurring themes emerged: familial conflict, the burden of expectations, and the struggle for autonomy. The tone is consistently tense and emotionally charged, reflecting Starlis's internal and external conflicts. My style tends to be descriptive, focusing on the characters' emotions and the intricate dynamics of their relationships.

Moving forward, I aim to delve deeper into Starlis's internal monologue, exploring her motivations and fears more intimately. This will add depth to her character and enhance the emotional resonance of her journey.

5. Seek Feedback and Be Open to Criticism

Exercise: Feedback Loop

- **Task:** Join a writing group or workshop. Share a piece of your writing and ask for specific feedback on your voice and style. Reflect on the feedback and consider how it aligns with your vision for your writing.
- **Goal:** To gain constructive criticism and refine your voice based on external perspectives.

Example:

Writing Group Session: Sharing an Excerpt from "The Fallen of Lite and Darke"

Shared Excerpt

As she entered the opulent throne room, Starlis carried herself with an air of unyielding dignity. Her gaze, unwavering and resolute, remained fixed on the queen, her mother, who sat enshrined upon her throne. Approaching the foot of the dais, Starlis confronted her mother's penetrating glare, noting her father standing just a shade behind the throne. His midnight black hair was as disheveled as ever, a stark contrast to the queen's meticulous aura, yet akin in the darkness that seemed to envelop him.

"Mother?" Starlis' voice cut through the thick air, a mix of formality and suppressed emotion.

"Shouldn't you be immersed in your studies? You have much to learn before you are deemed fit to ascend to this throne," came her mother's response, sharp as shattered glass, cutting through any pretense of maternal warmth.

Starlis internalized the sting of her mother's words, vowing to herself that she would one day be rid of that piercing, glass-like tone. She studied her mother's features intently, memorizing every detail—the unnaturally pale skin devoid of any luminescent shimmers, the hollowed silver eyes with mere flecks of gold, and the sheer dress that left little to the imagination. A dress that symbolized the transparency of her mother's disdain. Starlis felt a surge of loathing, deeper than any she had known before. Primitiva had always shouldered the burden of their collective resentment, but now, in her absence, the weight fell solely on Starlis' shoulders.

"Primitiva is gone," she announced, her voice carrying a mixture of accusation and concealed grief.

Queen Despina's reaction to Starlis's news was one of uncharacteristic horror. "Gone? What do you mean she's gone?" Her voice trembled with an emotion rarely displayed.

Starlis, surprised by this display of distress from her usually stoic mother, raised her hands in a gesture of pacification. It was a rarity in Lunaista, or any of the Star Cities for that matter, to witness such turmoil. "She's just vanished," Starlis explained, maintaining a calm and respectful tone despite the storm of emotions inside her. "I believe she chose the Void. Her disdain for the catacombs and her refusal to marry any prince from the Star Cities were well known. You're aware she always rebelled against the rules, Mother. And the idea of being a traditional mother was never in her plans."

Despina sank back into her crystal throne, a look of despair clouding her features. "Do you grasp the gravity of her actions? She's doomed our family... and your future."

Starlis had always perceived her mother as a heartless ruler, so this semblance of concern seemed almost theatrical. "Mother, the laws aren't as rigid as we've believed. The decree states that a tribute from the royal lineage must be offered before a new ruler ascends. It doesn't specify which family member."

"Your father is the only other option!" Despina exclaimed, her voice escalating into a scream.

Starlis, unable to mask her frustration, rolled her eyes. Her mother's demeanor was more akin to a petulant child than a sovereign. "If you continue to uphold this archaic tradition, then you are as responsible for what follows as Primitiva," she retorted. Turning her back on Despina, she added, "I must now prepare for my ascension. It's best not to dwell on this... We wouldn't want Primitiva's alleged dishonor to overshadow the coronation."

As she walked away, Starlis knew that the gossip and whispers that would inevitably follow held little significance for her. Her focus was elsewhere, on the daunting path that lay ahead.

Feedback from Writing Group

Feedback 1:

- **Comment:** "Your descriptions are very vivid and immersive, which is great for setting the scene. However, some parts feel a bit too dense, making it harder to follow the action."
- **Suggestion:** "Try to balance detailed descriptions with moments of action or dialogue to maintain the narrative flow."

Feedback 2:

- **Comment:** "The emotional tension between Starlis and her mother is palpable. I really felt the weight of their relationship."
- **Suggestion:** "Consider adding more internal monologue from Starlis to give readers deeper insight into her thoughts and motivations."

Feedback 3:

- **Comment:** "The dialogue is strong and characterizes the queen well. However, Starlis's reactions sometimes seem muted given the gravity of the situation."
- **Suggestion:** "Enhance Starlis's emotional responses to highlight her internal conflict more clearly."

Feedback 4:

- **Comment:** "The pacing is a bit slow at the beginning but picks up nicely towards the end."
- **Suggestion:** "You might want to start with a more dynamic scene or dialogue to hook the reader right away."

Reflective Journal Entry

Reflecting on the feedback received, I've gained several valuable insights into my writing:

Balancing Description and Action:

- **Insight:** While my descriptions are vivid, they can overwhelm the narrative flow.
- **Application:** I will work on interspersing detailed descriptions with more action and dialogue to keep the reader engaged.

Deepening Character Insight:

- **Insight:** Readers appreciated the emotional tension but wanted more internal perspective from Starlis.
- **Application:** I'll incorporate more of Starlis's internal monologue to provide a deeper understanding of her thoughts and feelings.

Enhancing Emotional Responses:

- **Insight:** Starlis's emotional responses need to be more pronounced.
- **Application:** I'll emphasize Starlis's reactions and internal conflicts to make her character more relatable and dynamic.

Pacing Improvements:

- o **Insight:** The pacing starts slow but improves towards the end.
- o **Application:** I'll consider starting with a more engaging scene or dialogue to capture the reader's attention from the beginning.

This feedback has been instrumental in helping me refine my voice and style. By incorporating these suggestions, I aim to create a more balanced, emotionally engaging, and dynamic narrative that resonates with readers.

6. Emphasize Your Strengths

Exercise: Strength Identification

- **Task:** Write a list of what you believe are your strengths as a writer (e.g., vivid descriptions, engaging dialogue). Then, write a piece that prominently features these strengths.
- **Goal:** To identify and highlight your unique strengths in your writing.

Example:

List of Strengths

1. **Vivid Descriptions:** I excel at creating detailed and immersive scenes that transport the reader into the world I've crafted.
2. **Engaging Dialogue:** My dialogue is natural and helps to define characters and their relationships.
3. **Emotional Depth:** I am adept at conveying the emotional undertones of a scene, making the reader feel the characters' experiences.
4. **Strong Characterization:** My characters are well-developed and multidimensional, each with their own distinct voice and personality.
5. **Narrative Flow:** I can weave a narrative that flows smoothly, keeping the reader engaged from start to finish.

Example Piece Featuring These Strengths

The sun was setting, casting a warm, golden glow over the ancient ruins of Azaria. Tall, weathered columns stood like silent sentinels, their surfaces etched with the stories of a forgotten civilization. The air was thick with the scent of blooming night jasmine, and the soft rustle of leaves whispered secrets carried on the evening breeze.

In the heart of the ruins, two figures stood facing each other. The first, a young woman named Lyra, had eyes that mirrored the fading light, filled with a mix of determination and sorrow. Her long, auburn hair cascaded over her shoulders, catching the last rays of the sun like a fiery halo. The second figure, an older man with a rugged, battle-worn appearance, was her mentor, Thorne.

"Are you sure about this, Lyra?" Thorne's voice was rough, yet it carried a note of tenderness that belied his gruff exterior. He watched her with a mixture of pride and concern, his hand resting on the hilt of his sword.

Lyra nodded, her gaze unwavering. "I have to do this, Thorne. For my family, for our people. The prophecy says that the one who holds the heart of the Phoenix can restore the balance."

Thorne sighed, his expression softening. "I know. But the path you're choosing is fraught with danger. The heart of the Phoenix is not just a legend; it's a curse as well."

Lyra stepped closer, her voice steady. "I understand the risks. But if I don't try, who will? This is my destiny, Thorne. I feel it in my bones."

Thorne's eyes searched hers, finding the resolute determination that had always defined her. "Very well. But promise me you'll be careful. The shadows that guard the heart are relentless."

A smile touched Lyra's lips, a flicker of warmth in the gathering twilight. "I promise. And thank you, Thorne. For everything."

The older man nodded, a silent acknowledgement of the bond they shared. As Lyra turned to leave, the ruins seemed to come alive, the shadows lengthening and the air growing cooler. She felt the weight of her task settling on her shoulders, but also the strength that came from knowing she was not alone.

With each step, Lyra's resolve hardened. The heart of the Phoenix awaited, and with it, the hope of a new dawn for her people. As the first stars appeared in the sky, she disappeared into the encroaching darkness, ready to face whatever trials lay ahead.

Reflection

This piece showcases my strengths as a writer. The vivid descriptions of the ancient ruins and the setting sun aim to immerse the reader in the scene. The engaging dialogue between Lyra and Thorne serves to develop their characters and reveal their deep bond. The emotional depth is highlighted through their exchange, conveying the gravity of Lyra's decision and Thorne's concern. Strong characterization is evident in Lyra's determined resolve and Thorne's protective nature. Finally, the narrative flow ensures that the scene transitions smoothly, maintaining the reader's interest and setting the stage for Lyra's journey.

By focusing on these strengths, I can create compelling and immersive stories that resonate deeply with my readers.

7. Let Go of Perfectionism

Exercise: Free Writing

- **Task:** Set a timer for 10 minutes and write continuously without editing or worrying about grammar or coherence. Focus on letting your thoughts flow freely.
- **Goal:** To overcome the pressure of perfectionism and embrace the creative process.

Example

The forest was alive with sounds of night, crickets chirping in a rythmick symphony that echoed thru the trees. The moonlight filtered through the dense canopy, casting silver patches on the forest floor. A soft breeze rustled the leaves, carrying with it the scent of pine and earth, a reminder of the wild untamed nature of the woods. In the middle of this serene chaos stood a small clearing, illuminated by a circle of glowing mushrooms that seemed to pulse with an inner light

Liora stood at the edge of the clearing, her heart pounding with a mix of excitement and trepidation. She had heard stories about the enchanted forest all her life, tales of ancient magic and mystical creatures that inhabited its depths. Tonight she was determined to uncover its secrets. Clutching her amulet tightly, she took a deep breath and stepped into the circle of light. Immediately, the air seemed to hum with energy, a palpable force that tingled on her skin and made her hair stand on end.

Suddenly the ground beneath her feet began to glow, intricate patterns of light spreading out in all directions like a spider's web. Liora watched in awe as the patterns formed symbols and runes she had never seen before, their meaning just out of reach, tantalizingly close yet frustratingly elusive. She could feel the magic coursing through her veins, a connection to something ancient and powerful, something that had been waiting for her for centuries.

As she stood there, mesmerized by the glowing runes, a figure emerged from the shadows. It was a tall, ethereal being with eyes that sparkled like starlight and hair that flowed like liquid silver. The being moved with a grace that was almost otherworldly, each step a dance, each movement a song. It stopped in front of Liora, its gaze piercing and yet strangely comforting

"Who are you?" Liora asked, her voice barely more than a whisper.

The being smiled, a soft, knowing smile that spoke of ages past and wisdom beyond comprehension. "I am the guardian of this forest," it said, its voice like the gentle rustle of leaves in the wind. "I have been waiting for you, Liora."

Liora's eyes widened in surprise. "You know my name?"

The guardian nodded. "Yes, I know much about you. You are the one destined to awaken the magic of this forest, to restore the balance that has been lost."

"But how?" Liora asked, feeling a mix of fear and exhilaration. "I'm just an ordinary girl. How can I possibly do that?"

The guardian reached out and touched Liora's amulet, and it began to glow with a light that matched the runes on the ground. "You have the heart of a true mage, Liora. The power lies within you. All you need to do is believe in yourself and let the magic guide you."

Liora looked down at the glowing amulet, feeling a surge of confidence she had never felt before. She nodded, determination filling her heart. "I will do it. I will restore the balance."

The guardian's smile widened. "Then the forest is in good hands." With that, the being began to fade, its form dissolving into a shower of sparkling light that danced around Liora before disappearing into the night.

Liora stood alone in the clearing, but she no longer felt afraid. She knew what she had to do, and she knew she had the power to do it. With a final look at the glowing runes, she turned and walked back into the forest, ready to embrace her destiny.

Reflection

Writing continuously for 10 minutes without worrying about perfection allowed me to tap into a raw and unfiltered flow of creativity. The story emerged organically, driven by the imagery and emotions I envisioned. This exercise helped me realize the importance of letting go and trusting the process, allowing the narrative to unfold naturally. Embracing imperfection can lead to unexpected and beautiful outcomes, fostering a more authentic and engaging voice in my writing.

8. Stay Patient and Persistent

Exercise: Writing Journey Timeline

- **Task:** Create a timeline of your writing journey, marking significant milestones, challenges, and achievements. Reflect on your growth and set future goals for developing your voice.
- **Goal:** To maintain perspective on your progress and stay motivated.

Example

Writing Journey Timeline

2010: The Beginning

- **Milestone:** Started writing short stories in high school.
- **Challenge:** Overcoming self-doubt and finding the courage to share my work.
- **Achievement:** Won a local writing contest with my story "The Enchanted Forest."

Reflection: This was the time when I discovered my love for storytelling. Winning the contest gave me the confidence to pursue writing more seriously.

2013: College Years

- **Milestone:** Enrolled in Creative Writing classes at university.
- **Challenge:** Balancing academic workload with personal writing projects.
- **Achievement:** Published my first short story in the university literary magazine.

Reflection: College was a period of intense learning and growth. I received constructive feedback from professors and peers, which helped refine my voice.

2016: First Novel Attempt

- **Milestone:** Started writing my first novel, "Whispers of the Past."
- **Challenge:** Struggling with writer's block and plot development.
- **Achievement:** Completed the first draft after a year of persistent effort.

Reflection: Writing a novel was a monumental task. The process taught me the importance of persistence and the value of a structured writing routine.

2018: Entering the Publishing World

- **Milestone:** Finished editing "Whispers of the Past" and began querying agents.
- **Challenge:** Facing numerous rejections and maintaining motivation.
- **Achievement:** Received positive feedback from an agent, which led to a publishing contract.

Reflection: The rejections were tough, but they taught me resilience. Getting a publishing contract was a significant validation of my hard work and dedication.

2020: Book Release and Beyond

- **Milestone:** "Whispers of the Past" published and launched.
- **Challenge:** Navigating book promotion and connecting with readers during the pandemic.
- **Achievement:** Book became a bestseller in its genre on release.

Reflection: The success of my first book was incredibly rewarding. Engaging with readers and hearing their feedback was motivating and fulfilling.

2022: Expanding Horizons

- **Milestone:** Began writing a fantasy series, "The Fallen of Lite and Darke."
- **Challenge:** Experimenting with a new genre and building a complex fantasy world.
- **Achievement:** Completed the first book in the series and received positive early reviews.

Reflection: Transitioning to fantasy was both exciting and challenging. It allowed me to explore new creative avenues and grow as a writer.

Future Goals

Continue Developing My Fantasy Series:

- o Complete the next two books in "The Fallen of Lite and Darke" series.
- o Explore deeper character development and intricate plot twists.

Enhance My Writing Skills:

- o Attend writing workshops and seminars to learn from other authors.
- o Experiment with different writing styles and techniques to further refine my voice.

Engage with the Writing Community:

- o Participate in writer's conferences and online forums.
- o Mentor aspiring writers and share my journey to inspire others.

Expand My Publishing Portfolio:

- o Write and publish a non-fiction book on the writing process and overcoming challenges.
- o Explore self-publishing options for smaller projects and anthologies.

Reflection

Creating this timeline has been a powerful reminder of my journey and growth as a writer. Each milestone, challenge, and achievement has shaped my voice and strengthened my resolve. By setting future goals, I aim to continue evolving and contributing to the literary world. Staying patient and persistent has been key to my success, and I am excited for the road ahead.

9. Reflect on Your Journey

Exercise: Comparative Analysis

- **Task:** Select a piece of writing from a year ago and compare it to a recent piece. Write a reflection on how your voice has evolved and what you have learned about yourself as a writer.
- **Goal:** To recognize and appreciate your development over time.

Example:

Writing Piece from a Year Ago

Excerpt from "The Enchanted Woods" (2023)

The forest was a place of mystery and wonder. Tall trees loomed overhead, their branches intertwining to form a dense canopy that blocked out the sunlight. The air was cool and damp, filled with the earthy scent of moss and fallen leaves. In the heart of the forest, a small stream trickled over rocks, its gentle murmur a soothing backdrop to the otherwise silent woods.

Lara moved cautiously through the underbrush, her senses alert to every sound and movement. She had heard stories of the enchanted woods, tales of magic and danger that kept most people away. But Lara was determined to find the ancient tree that was said to hold the secret to eternal life. She knew the journey would be perilous, but she was prepared for whatever lay ahead.

As she approached the stream, Lara noticed something unusual. The water, usually clear and sparkling, was tinged with a faint golden hue. She knelt beside it, reaching out to touch the shimmering liquid. As soon as her fingers made contact, a jolt of energy surged through her, and she knew she had found something extraordinary.

Recent Writing Piece

Excerpt from "The Fallen of Lite and Darke" (2024)

The forest was alive with the symphony of night, crickets chirping in a rhythmic chorus that echoed through the towering trees. Moonlight filtered through the dense canopy, casting dappled silver patches on the forest floor. A soft breeze rustled the leaves, carrying the scent of pine and earth, a reminder of the untamed wilderness.

In the midst of this serene chaos, a small clearing bathed in the glow of luminescent mushrooms pulsed with an inner light. Liora stood at the edge, her heart pounding with a mix of excitement and trepidation. She had heard countless tales of the enchanted forest, stories of ancient magic and mystical beings that dwelled within its depths. Tonight, she would uncover its secrets.

Clutching her amulet tightly, Liora took a deep breath and stepped into the circle of light. The air hummed with energy, a palpable force that tingled on her skin. Suddenly, the ground beneath her feet began to glow, intricate patterns of light spreading out like a spider's web. Liora watched in awe as the symbols and runes formed, their meaning just out of reach, tantalizingly close yet frustratingly elusive.

A figure emerged from the shadows, an ethereal being with eyes that sparkled like starlight and hair that flowed like liquid silver. The being moved with a grace that seemed almost otherworldly, each step a dance, each movement a song. It stopped before Liora, its gaze both piercing and comforting.

"Who are you?" Liora whispered.

The being smiled, a knowing smile that spoke of ages past and wisdom beyond comprehension. "I am the guardian of this forest. I have been waiting for you, Liora."

Reflection

Comparing these two pieces, I notice significant evolution in my writing style and voice over the past year.

Descriptive Detail:

1. **2023:** My descriptions were functional but lacked depth and vivid imagery. I focused more on setting the scene rather than immersing the reader in it.
2. **2024:** My recent writing uses more vivid and sensory details, creating a more immersive and atmospheric setting. The forest in "The Fallen of Lite and Darke" feels alive and dynamic, engaging the reader's senses more fully.

Character Development:

1. **2023:** Lara's character is introduced with a clear goal, but her emotions and inner thoughts are not deeply explored.
2. **2024:** Liora's character is portrayed with a mix of excitement and trepidation, providing a more nuanced and relatable emotional landscape. Her interaction with the environment and the guardian adds depth to her character.

Narrative Flow:

1. **2023:** The narrative in "The Enchanted Woods" is straightforward and linear, focusing on plot progression.
2. **2024:** The narrative in "The Fallen of Lite and Darke" is more fluid and layered, with a balance between action, description, and introspection. The pacing varies to enhance the mood and tension.

Voice and Style:

1. **2023:** My voice was more tentative, sticking to conventional storytelling methods without much experimentation.

2. **2024:** My voice has become more confident and distinctive. I'm experimenting with rhythm and cadence, creating a lyrical and evocative narrative style that enhances the fantasy genre.

Lessons Learned

- **Embrace Sensory Details:** Descriptive language can transform a setting from a static backdrop into a vibrant, integral part of the story.
- **Develop Characters Emotionally:** Deepening the emotional portrayal of characters makes them more relatable and engaging.
- **Balance Narrative Elements:** A mix of action, description, and introspection creates a richer and more compelling narrative.
- **Cultivate a Distinctive Voice:** Confidence in experimenting with style and voice can lead to a more unique and memorable storytelling approach.

Future Goals

1. **Continue Enhancing Descriptive Language:** Focus on incorporating more sensory details to create immersive settings.
2. **Deepen Emotional Characterization:** Explore characters' inner worlds and emotional journeys more thoroughly.
3. **Experiment with Narrative Structure:** Play with different narrative techniques to keep the storytelling dynamic and engaging.
4. **Refine and Evolve Voice:** Continue developing a distinctive narrative voice that resonates with readers and enhances the genre.

Recognizing my progress over the past year has been encouraging and motivating. It reminds me that writing is an ongoing journey of growth and discovery. By reflecting on my development, I can set purposeful goals to continue evolving as a writer.

 By embracing your authentic self, experimenting with different styles, reading widely, writing regularly, seeking feedback, emphasizing your strengths, letting go of perfectionism, staying patient, and reflecting on your journey, you will discover and hone a writing voice that is unmistakably your own. Your unique voice is your greatest asset as a writer, and cultivating it will make your work stand out and resonate deeply with your readers.

Exercises for Developing a Consistent Writing Routine

1. Set Clear Goals

Exercise: Define Your Writing Objectives

- **Task:** Write down your specific writing goals. For example, aim to write 500 words per day, complete a chapter each week, or dedicate 1 hour to writing daily.
- **Goal:** To establish clear and achievable objectives that provide direction and motivation.

2. Establish a Writing Schedule

Exercise: Create Your Ideal Writing Schedule

- **Task:** Choose a consistent time each day for writing. Record your chosen time and commit to writing at that time daily for the next two weeks.
- **Goal:** To develop a habit of writing at the same time every day, making it a natural part of your routine.

3. Create a Dedicated Writing Space

Exercise: Design Your Writing Environment

- **Task:** Identify a quiet, comfortable spot for writing. Personalize this space with items that inspire you, such as quotes, plants, or favorite books.
- **Goal:** To create a dedicated space that enhances focus and creativity.

4. Minimize Distractions

Exercise: Implement Distraction-Blocking Techniques

- **Task:** Turn off notifications on your devices, close unnecessary tabs, and inform others of your writing time to minimize interruptions.
- **Goal:** To create a distraction-free environment that allows you to concentrate fully on writing.

5. Warm Up with Writing Prompts

Exercise: Daily Writing Prompt Warm-Up

- **Task:** Spend 10 minutes each day responding to a random writing prompt before starting your main writing project. Use prompts like "Describe a stormy night" or "What if animals could talk?"
- **Goal:** To ease into writing sessions and stimulate creativity.

6. Set Realistic Expectations

Exercise: Reflect on Your Daily Writing Sessions

- **Task:** At the end of each writing session, jot down what you accomplished, whether it was a few paragraphs or several pages.
- **Goal:** To accept and celebrate your daily progress, no matter how small, and to maintain a positive mindset.

7. Track Your Progress

Exercise: Maintain a Writing Journal

- **Task:** Keep a daily record of your word count, time spent writing, and any significant thoughts or breakthroughs. Review this journal weekly.
- **Goal:** To track progress, identify productivity patterns, and make necessary adjustments to your routine.

8. Develop a Pre-Writing Ritual

Exercise: Establish a Consistent Pre-Writing Routine

- **Task:** Choose a simple activity to perform before each writing session, such as making a cup of tea, listening to calming music, or stretching.
- **Goal:** To create a mental transition that prepares you for focused writing.

9. Stay Flexible and Adaptable

Exercise: Plan for Flexibility

- **Task:** Identify potential disruptions to your writing routine and develop a backup plan. For instance, if you miss a morning session, plan a shorter session in the evening.
- **Goal:** To adapt to unexpected changes without getting discouraged and to maintain long-term consistency.

10. Seek Accountability and Support

Exercise: Find an Accountability Partner

- **Task:** Share your writing goals with a friend, family member, or writing group. Schedule regular check-ins to discuss your progress and challenges.
- **Goal:** To stay motivated and receive encouragement from others, enhancing your commitment to your writing routine.

Example Timeline for Implementing the Exercises

Week 1

- **Day 1-3:** Set clear goals and create your writing schedule.
- **Day 4-6:** Design your writing space and implement distraction-blocking techniques.
- **Day 7:** Start your writing prompt warm-up exercises.

Week 2

- **Day 1-3:** Continue writing prompts and reflect on daily writing sessions.
- **Day 4-6:** Begin tracking progress in your writing journal and establish a pre-writing ritual.
- **Day 7:** Identify potential disruptions and develop backup plans.

Week 3

- **Day 1-3:** Seek an accountability partner and schedule check-ins.
- **Day 4-6:** Review your writing journal and make any necessary adjustments to your routine.
- **Day 7:** Reflect on your progress and celebrate your achievements.

By following these exercises and timeline, you will develop a consistent writing routine that integrates seamlessly into your daily life, fostering steady progress and growth as a writer.

Exercises for Overcoming Writer's Block

1. Change Your Environment

Exercise: Writing in a New Place

- **Task:** Choose a different location to write, such as a café, library, park, or a different room in your home. Spend at least one writing session in this new environment and note any changes in your creativity or productivity.
- **Goal:** To stimulate your senses and spark new ideas by altering your writing surroundings.

2. Freewriting

Exercise: 10-Minute Freewriting Session

- **Task:** Set a timer for 10 minutes. Write continuously without worrying about grammar, punctuation, or coherence. Let your thoughts flow freely, and don't stop writing until the timer goes off.

- **Goal:** To bypass your internal editor and unlock new ideas, often leading to surprising and inspiring results.

3. Use Writing Prompts

Exercise: Prompt-Driven Writing

- **Task:** Choose a writing prompt and write a short piece based on it. Examples of prompts include:
    - Describe a character who has a secret they're desperate to keep.
    - Write about a place where time stands still.
    - Imagine a conversation between two people who speak different languages.

- **Goal:** To provide a starting point that helps you get past the initial hurdle of writer's block.

4. Set Small, Achievable Goals

Exercise: Mini-Goals for Writing Sessions

- **Task:** Set a small goal for your writing session, such as writing a single paragraph, describing a character, or crafting one compelling sentence. Achieve this mini-goal before moving on to larger tasks.
- **Goal:** To make writing less overwhelming and build momentum through small successes.

5. Read and Recharge

Exercise: Reading for Inspiration

- **Task:** Take a break from writing and read something that inspires you—a novel, a poem, an article, or even a blog post. Spend at least 15-20 minutes reading and note any new ideas or insights that arise.
- **Goal:** To recharge your creativity and gain new perspectives that might spark your own writing.

6. Engage in a Different Creative Activity

Exercise: Creative Break

- **Task:** Step away from writing and engage in a different creative activity, such as drawing, painting, playing music, or cooking. Spend at least 30 minutes on this activity and observe any changes in your mindset.
- **Goal:** To stimulate your brain in new ways and approach your writing with a fresh perspective.

7. Establish a Writing Ritual

Exercise: Create a Pre-Writing Ritual

- **Task:** Choose a simple activity to perform before each writing session, such as making a cup of tea, listening to a specific playlist, or spending a few minutes meditating. Perform this ritual consistently before you start writing.
- **Goal:** To create a mental transition that signals to your brain it's time to write, making it easier to get started.

8. Embrace the Imperfection

Exercise: Imperfection Writing

- **Task:** Write a short piece with the intention of it being imperfect. Focus on getting words down without self-criticism. Accept that this piece will be rough and that's okay.
- **Goal:** To overcome the fear of imperfection and allow yourself to write freely without judgment.

9. Take Breaks and Practice Self-Care

Exercise: Scheduled Breaks

- **Task:** Schedule regular breaks during your writing sessions. For example, write for 25 minutes, then take a 5-minute break. During breaks, engage in a relaxing activity like stretching, walking, or deep breathing.

- **Goal:** To maintain mental and physical well-being, which is crucial for long-term productivity and creativity.

10. Reflect and Reconnect with Your Why

Exercise: Reflection Journal

- **Task:** Spend 10 minutes writing about why you started writing in the first place. Reflect on your passion, the stories you want to tell, and the impact you hope to make. Keep this journal entry visible as a reminder.
- **Goal:** To reignite your inspiration and reconnect with your motivation for writing.

11. Break Down Your Project

Exercise: Project Breakdown

- **Task:** Create an outline or a to-do list that breaks your writing project into specific sections or chapters. Focus on completing one small section at a time.
- **Goal:** To make your project less intimidating and maintain a sense of progress and achievement.

12. Seek Support from Other Writers

Exercise: Join a Writing Group

- **Task:** Join a writing group, attend a workshop, or participate in an online forum. Share your struggles and successes, and seek encouragement from fellow writers.
- **Goal:** To feel supported and motivated by connecting with others who understand the challenges of writer's block.

By incorporating these exercises into your routine, you can overcome writer's block and maintain your productivity. Remember, writer's block is a temporary hurdle, not a permanent roadblock. With the right approach, you can break through and continue making progress on your writing journey.

Exercises for Effective Editing and Revising

1. Enhancing Clarity and Coherence

Exercise: Outline and Rearrange

- **Task:** Create a detailed outline of your manuscript. Summarize each chapter or section in a few sentences. Identify any areas where the flow of ideas is unclear or where the narrative could be more logically organized. Rearrange sections as needed to improve coherence.
- **Goal:** To ensure that your manuscript is logically structured and that the narrative flows smoothly.

Example:

Detailed Outline Example for "The Enchanted Forest"

Chapter 1: The Call to Adventure

Summary:
Liora, a young villager, hears rumors about the magical Enchanted Forest. She is intrigued and feels a strong pull to explore it, despite warnings from her family and friends.

Notes:

- Introduce Liora and her village.
- Establish the mystery and allure of the Enchanted Forest.
- Highlight the initial resistance and concern from her family.

Chapter 2: Entering the Forest

Summary:
Despite her fears, Liora decides to venture into the Enchanted Forest. She encounters various magical creatures and experiences the forest's enchantment firsthand.

Notes:

- Describe the transition from village to forest.
- Introduce the setting of the forest and its magical elements.
- Show Liora's initial reactions and interactions with the creatures.

Chapter 3: The Guardian of the Forest

Summary:
Liora meets the Guardian of the Forest, an ethereal being who reveals that Liora has a special connection to the forest. The Guardian explains the forest's history and its current plight.

Notes:

- Introduce the Guardian and their wisdom.
- Provide backstory about the forest and its significance.
- Foreshadow Liora's role in the forest's future.

Chapter 4: Trials and Tribulations

Summary:
Liora faces various challenges within the forest that test her courage and determination. She learns more about her abilities and the forest's secrets.

Notes:

- Detail the specific trials Liora encounters.
- Show character growth through overcoming obstacles.
- Deepen the mystery and stakes.

Chapter 5: The Heart of the Forest

Summary:
Liora discovers the Heart of the Forest, a powerful source of magic. She must protect it from dark forces seeking to corrupt it.

Notes:

- Describe the Heart of the Forest and its significance.
- Introduce the antagonists and their motives.
- Build tension towards the climax.

Chapter 6: The Final Confrontation

Summary:
Liora faces the dark forces in a climactic battle to protect the Heart of the Forest. With the help of the Guardian and the forest creatures, she emerges victorious.

Notes:

- Detail the final battle and its stakes.
- Highlight teamwork and the culmination of Liora's growth.
- Resolve major conflicts.

Chapter 7: Returning Home

Summary:
Liora returns to her village, forever changed by her journey. She shares her experiences and newfound wisdom, inspiring others.

Notes:

- Show Liora's return and the impact on her village.
- Reflect on the journey's lessons and Liora's transformation.
- End with a hopeful outlook for the future.

Identifying Areas for Improvement

Observations:

Chapter Flow:

- The transition between some chapters feels abrupt, particularly between Chapter 2 (Entering the Forest) and Chapter 3 (The Guardian of the Forest).
- The initial introduction of the antagonists in Chapter 5 (The Heart of the Forest) seems too late in the story.

Character Development:

- Liora's growth and development need more emphasis between Chapters 4 (Trials and Tribulations) and 5 (The Heart of the Forest).

Narrative Clarity:

- The backstory provided by the Guardian in Chapter 3 might overwhelm the reader with information all at once.

Rearranging for Improved Coherence

Revised Outline

Chapter 1: The Call to Adventure

- Liora, a young villager, hears rumors about the magical Enchanted Forest. She is intrigued and feels a strong pull to explore it, despite warnings from her family and friends.

Chapter 2: Entering the Forest

- Despite her fears, Liora decides to venture into the Enchanted Forest. She encounters various magical creatures and experiences the forest's enchantment firsthand.

Chapter 3: The Guardian's Revelation

- Liora meets the Guardian of the Forest, an ethereal being who reveals that Liora has a special connection to the forest. The Guardian explains some of the forest's history and hints at Liora's role.

Chapter 4: Trials and Tribulations

- Liora faces various challenges within the forest that test her courage and determination. She learns more about her abilities and the forest's secrets.

Chapter 5: Introducing the Antagonists

- Liora encounters the dark forces seeking to corrupt the Heart of the Forest. She learns about their motives and the impending danger.

Chapter 6: The Heart of the Forest

- Liora discovers the Heart of the Forest, a powerful source of magic. She must protect it from the dark forces.

Chapter 7: The Final Confrontation

- Liora faces the dark forces in a climactic battle to protect the Heart of the Forest. With the help of the Guardian and the forest creatures, she emerges victorious.

Chapter 8: Returning Home

- Liora returns to her village, forever changed by her journey. She shares her experiences and newfound wisdom, inspiring others.

Reflection

By rearranging the chapters, the narrative flow is improved, making the story more coherent. The introduction of the antagonists earlier helps build tension and prepares the reader for the climax. Additionally, spreading out the backstory provided by the Guardian prevents information overload and maintains reader engagement. This revised structure enhances clarity and coherence, ensuring a smoother reading experience.

2. Improving Language and Style

Exercise: Sentence Variation and Vocabulary Enhancement

- **Task:** Choose a chapter and highlight sentences that are repetitive in structure or use vague language. Rewrite these sentences, varying the structure and incorporating more precise vocabulary. Pay attention to rhythm and tone.
- **Goal:** To refine your language, enhance your writing style, and ensure your unique voice shines through.

Example:

Original Excerpt from Chapter 2: Entering the Forest

Liora walked into the forest. She saw the tall trees. The leaves rustled in the wind. The forest was dark and mysterious. She felt a sense of excitement and fear. She continued walking deeper. She noticed strange plants and animals. The path was narrow and winding. She heard sounds all around her. She felt like she was being watched.

Highlighted Sentences for Revision

1. **Repetitive Structure:** Liora walked into the forest. She saw the tall trees.
2. **Vague Language:** The forest was dark and mysterious. She felt a sense of excitement and fear.
3. **Repetitive Structure:** She continued walking deeper. She noticed strange plants and animals.

4. **Vague Language:** The path was narrow and winding. She heard sounds all around her. She felt like she was being watched.

Revised Excerpt with Sentence Variation and Vocabulary Enhancement

As Liora stepped into the forest, towering trees loomed overhead, their branches intertwining to form a canopy that filtered the sunlight into dappled shadows. The leaves rustled softly in the breeze, whispering secrets of the ancient woods. An aura of mystery and darkness enveloped her, sending shivers down her spine as a thrilling blend of excitement and trepidation coursed through her veins.

Venturing further, she marveled at the exotic flora and fauna that thrived in this hidden world. The path ahead twisted and turned, a narrow ribbon of earth barely visible amid the dense undergrowth. Strange sounds echoed from all directions, making her acutely aware of her surroundings. The sensation of unseen eyes following her every move intensified, heightening her awareness of the forest's enigmatic presence.

Reflection

Before Revision:

- **Repetitive Structure:** The original sentences followed a simple and repetitive structure, which made the narrative feel monotonous.
- **Vague Language:** Words like "dark," "mysterious," "excitement," and "fear" were used without providing vivid imagery or deeper emotional context.

After Revision:

- **Sentence Variation:** The revised sentences vary in length and structure, creating a more dynamic and engaging rhythm. For example, "As Liora stepped into the forest, towering trees loomed overhead" combines descriptive imagery with action.
- **Precise Vocabulary:** The use of specific and evocative language, such as "towering trees," "dappled shadows," "aura of mystery," and "thrilling blend of excitement and trepidation," enhances the vividness and emotional depth of the narrative.
- **Enhanced Rhythm and Tone:** The new passage flows more smoothly, capturing the reader's attention with its rhythmic and descriptive quality.

This exercise demonstrates how sentence variation and vocabulary enhancement can significantly improve the language and style of your writing. By paying attention to these elements, you can ensure that your unique voice shines through, creating a more compelling and polished manuscript.

3. Correcting Grammar and Punctuation

Exercise: Grammar and Punctuation Review

- **Task:** Select a section of your manuscript and review it specifically for grammatical errors and punctuation mistakes. Use a grammar-checking tool for an initial pass, then manually review it, reading aloud to catch any awkward phrasing or overlooked errors.
- **Goal:** To eliminate grammatical errors and punctuation mistakes, ensuring a polished and professional manuscript.

Example:

Original Excerpt from Chapter 3: The Guardian's Revelation

Liora couldnt believe her eyes. The Guardian, who she had heard about in legends, stood before her. "You are the chosen one," the Guardian said, its voice echoing through the forest "I have been waiting for you".

"Why me?" Liora asked, she felt a mix of fear and excitement.

"The forest has chosen you" replied the Guardian "You possess the heart of a true mage."

Liora's heart pounded in her chest, she had always known she was different but she never expected this. She reached out hesitantly, touching the Guardian's outstretched hand.

"You must protect the heart of the forest" the Guardian continued. "It is the source of all our magic".

Initial Pass with Grammar-Checking Tool

Corrected Excerpt:

Liora couldn't believe her eyes. The Guardian, whom she had heard about in legends, stood before her. "You are the chosen one," the Guardian said, its voice echoing through the forest. "I have been waiting for you."

"Why me?" Liora asked. She felt a mix of fear and excitement.

"The forest has chosen you," replied the Guardian. "You possess the heart of a true mage."

Liora's heart pounded in her chest. She had always known she was different, but she never expected this. She reached out hesitantly, touching the Guardian's outstretched hand.

"You must protect the heart of the forest," the Guardian continued. "It is the source of all our magic."

Manual Review and Reading Aloud

Revised and Polished Excerpt:

Liora couldn't believe her eyes. The Guardian, whom she had heard about in legends, stood before her. "You are the chosen one," the Guardian said, its voice echoing through the forest. "I have been waiting for you."

"Why me?" Liora asked. She felt a mix of fear and excitement.

"The forest has chosen you," replied the Guardian. "You possess the heart of a true mage."

Liora's heart pounded in her chest. She had always known she was different, but she never expected this. Hesitantly, she reached out and touched the Guardian's outstretched hand.

"You must protect the heart of the forest," the Guardian continued. "It is the source of all our magic."

Reflection

Before Revision:

- **Grammatical Errors:** Incorrect contractions ("couldnt"), misused relative pronoun ("who" instead of "whom"), and comma splices.
- **Punctuation Mistakes:** Missing periods, incorrect placement of commas and quotation marks, and lack of punctuation in dialogue.
- **Awkward Phrasing:** The sentence structure in some places felt clumsy, affecting the flow of the narrative.

After Revision:

- **Grammatical Corrections:** Fixed contractions, used the correct relative pronoun, and corrected comma splices.
- **Punctuation Improvements:** Added missing periods, corrected the placement of commas and quotation marks, and ensured punctuation in dialogue was accurate.
- **Enhanced Flow:** Adjusted phrasing for better readability and smoother narrative flow.

By using a grammar-checking tool and performing a manual review, the excerpt was polished to eliminate grammatical errors and punctuation mistakes. Reading the passage aloud helped catch awkward phrasings and ensure the text flowed naturally. This exercise highlights the importance of meticulous editing to produce a professional and polished manuscript.

4. Strengthening Character and Plot Development

Exercise: Character and Plot Analysis

- **Task:** Create detailed profiles for your main characters, including their motivations, conflicts, and growth throughout the story. Outline your plot, noting any inconsistencies or plot holes. Revise your manuscript to deepen character development and strengthen plotlines.
- **Goal:** To enhance the emotional depth and narrative complexity of your story, making it more compelling for readers.

Example:

Character Profiles

Main Character: Liora

Motivations:

- Discover her unique abilities and purpose.
- Protect the Enchanted Forest and its magical heart.

- Prove her worth to herself and her village.

Conflicts:

- Internal conflict about her identity and capabilities.
- External conflict with dark forces threatening the forest.
- Relational conflict with her family and the village elders who doubt her.

Growth:

- Starts as a curious and somewhat insecure girl.
- Gains confidence and self-assurance as she overcomes challenges.
- Becomes a determined and wise protector of the forest, understanding her role in its preservation.

Supporting Character: The Guardian

Motivations:

- Preserve the magic and balance of the Enchanted Forest.
- Guide and support Liora in her journey.

Conflicts:

- Struggles with the limitations of its ethereal form in directly intervening.
- Conflict with the dark forces that seek to corrupt the forest.

Growth:

- Begins as a distant, almost mythical figure.
- Develops a closer bond with Liora, becoming more emotionally involved.
- Learns to trust Liora's judgment and strength.

Antagonist: Dark Sorcerer

Motivations:

- Gain control over the magical heart of the forest.
- Use the forest's power to dominate other realms.

Conflicts:

- Direct conflict with Liora and the Guardian.
- Internal conflict driven by a lust for power and a fear of failure.

Growth:

- Starts as a menacing but one-dimensional villain.
- Develops a backstory revealing past betrayals and a misguided belief in their actions.
- Shows moments of vulnerability, making the character more complex.

Plot Outline and Analysis

Original Outline

Introduction:

- Liora hears rumors about the Enchanted Forest.
- Introduces her village, family, and initial conflicts.

Entering the Forest:

- Liora decides to explore the forest.
- Encounters magical creatures.

Meeting the Guardian:

- Liora meets the Guardian.
- Receives her quest to protect the forest.

Trials and Tribulations:

- Faces various challenges.
- Grows in confidence and ability.

Discovering the Heart:

- Finds the Heart of the Forest.
- Learns about the dark forces.

Confronting the Dark Sorcerer:

- Battles the antagonist.
- Protects the Heart.

Resolution:

- Returns home transformed.
- Shares her experiences with the village.

Identified Plot Holes and Inconsistencies

Inconsistent Motivations:

- Liora's motivations aren't clearly established early on.
- The Dark Sorcerer's backstory and reasons for seeking the Heart are vague.

Character Interactions:

- The relationship between Liora and the Guardian lacks depth.
- The Dark Sorcerer's conflict with Liora feels superficial.

Plot Holes:

- How Liora discovers specific knowledge about the Heart and its significance is unclear.
- The Guardian's limitations and abilities are not well-defined.

Revised Plot Outline

Introduction:

- Liora, feeling out of place in her village, is drawn to the mysterious Enchanted Forest.
- Establish her family's concern and the village elders' skepticism.

Entering the Forest:

- Liora's curiosity and need to prove herself lead her to the forest.
- Encounters both enchanting and dangerous elements, illustrating the forest's dual nature.

Meeting the Guardian:

- The Guardian initially appears distant but reveals the forest's history and Liora's connection to it.
- Sets clear stakes and foreshadows the coming conflict.

Trials and Tribulations:

- Liora faces both physical and emotional challenges.
- Interactions with forest creatures and the Guardian deepen her understanding of herself and her mission.

Discovering the Heart:

- Liora uncovers the Heart's location through a combination of intuition and guidance from the Guardian.
- Learns about the Dark Sorcerer's past and motivations, adding complexity to the antagonist.

Confronting the Dark Sorcerer:

- A climactic battle where Liora uses her newfound skills and wisdom.
- The Guardian provides crucial support, emphasizing their growing bond.

Resolution:

- Liora returns home, her transformation evident to all.
- She shares her journey's lessons, inspiring change and growth in her village.

Reflection

Before Revision:

- **Character Development:** Liora's motivations and growth were not fully fleshed out. The Guardian and Dark Sorcerer lacked depth.
- **Plot Consistency:** Some plot points were unclear or poorly developed, leading to confusion about characters' actions and motivations.
- **Narrative Depth:** The interactions between characters felt superficial, and the emotional stakes were not high enough.

After Revision:

- **Enhanced Motivations and Growth:** Liora's journey is more personal and emotionally driven. The Guardian and Dark Sorcerer are given more depth and backstory.
- **Clearer Plot:** The revised outline addresses inconsistencies and clarifies character motivations and actions.
- **Increased Emotional Depth:** The relationships between characters are more developed, and the stakes are higher, making the narrative more compelling.

By creating detailed character profiles and revising the plot outline, the manuscript gains emotional depth and narrative complexity, making the story more engaging and impactful for readers.

5. Eliminating Redundancies and Repetition

Exercise: Redundancy and Repetition Elimination

- **Task:** Read through a chapter and identify any repetitive ideas, phrases, or descriptions. Highlight these sections and rewrite them to eliminate redundancy. Ensure that each word, sentence, and paragraph serves a purpose and contributes to the overall narrative or argument.
- **Goal:** To streamline your manuscript, enhancing its readability and keeping readers engaged.

Example:

Original Excerpt from Chapter 4: Trials and Tribulations

Liora walked through the forest, feeling the dense underbrush beneath her feet. The trees were tall and their branches formed a thick canopy overhead. She felt a sense of excitement and fear as she ventured deeper. The forest was dark and mysterious, and she could hear the rustling of leaves and the distant call of an owl. Every step she took made a crunching sound on the forest floor. Liora had never been this deep in the forest before, and she felt a mixture of fear and excitement.

As she moved forward, she noticed strange, glowing plants. The plants were glowing with an eerie light. She had never seen such plants before. The glowing plants made the forest seem even more magical and mysterious. She felt a sense of awe and wonder as she looked at the glowing plants. Liora continued walking, her heart pounding with excitement and fear. She was determined to uncover the secrets of the forest.

Highlighted Redundancies and Repetition

Redundant Descriptions:

1. "The trees were tall and their branches formed a thick canopy overhead."

2. "The forest was dark and mysterious."
3. "Every step she took made a crunching sound on the forest floor."
4. "Liora had never been this deep in the forest before, and she felt a mixture of fear and excitement."

Repetitive Phrases:

1. "feeling the dense underbrush beneath her feet"
2. "a sense of excitement and fear"
3. "glowing plants"
4. "The glowing plants made the forest seem even more magical and mysterious."
5. "She felt a sense of awe and wonder as she looked at the glowing plants."

Revised Excerpt with Redundancies and Repetition Eliminated

Liora navigated the dense underbrush, the tall trees forming a thick canopy overhead, casting the forest in perpetual twilight. Each step she took echoed with the crunch of leaves and twigs underfoot, a reminder of the untamed wilderness surrounding her. A blend of excitement and fear coursed through her as she ventured deeper into the unknown.

Suddenly, her path was illuminated by an eerie glow. Strange plants, unlike any she had seen before, emitted a soft, otherworldly light. These luminescent flora added to the forest's magical aura, filling her with awe and wonder. Determined to uncover the secrets hidden within, Liora pressed on, her heart pounding with anticipation.

Reflection

Before Revision:

- **Redundant Descriptions:** The original passage repeatedly described the forest's attributes, such as its darkness, mystery, and the sounds of Liora's footsteps.
- **Repetitive Phrases:** Phrases like "a sense of excitement and fear" and "glowing plants" were overused, diminishing their impact.

After Revision:

- **Eliminated Redundancies:** Combined similar descriptions to avoid repetition, creating a more concise and engaging narrative.
- **Streamlined Phrases:** Reduced repetitive phrases, ensuring each sentence added new information or advanced the narrative.

By eliminating redundancies and repetition, the revised excerpt is more streamlined, enhancing readability and keeping the reader engaged. Each word, sentence, and paragraph now serves a distinct purpose, contributing to a more polished and compelling manuscript.

6. Incorporating Feedback

Exercise: Feedback Implementation

- **Task:** Share a section of your manuscript with trusted peers, beta readers, or professional editors. Ask for specific feedback on areas you are unsure about. Incorporate their constructive criticism and make revisions accordingly.
- **Goal:** To see your manuscript from different perspectives and address issues you might have overlooked.

Example:

Original Excerpt from Chapter 5: The Heart of the Forest

Liora stood before the Heart of the Forest, a glowing crystal pulsing with vibrant energy. She felt a deep connection to it, as if it were calling out to her. The dark sorcerer appeared suddenly, his eyes fixed on the crystal. "You cannot stop me," he sneered. Liora's heart pounded as she raised her hand, a shield of light forming around her. The sorcerer laughed and launched a bolt of dark energy at her. Liora deflected it with her shield, but she felt her strength waning.

Feedback from Beta Readers

Beta Reader 1:

- **Comment:** "The confrontation with the dark sorcerer feels rushed. Can you expand on the tension and stakes leading up to this moment?"
- **Suggestion:** "Add more details about Liora's feelings and the environment to build suspense."

Beta Reader 2:

- **Comment:** "Liora's shield appears too abruptly. It would be more impactful if you showed her struggling to summon it."
- **Suggestion:** "Show her internal struggle and the effort it takes to form the shield."

Beta Reader 3:

- **Comment:** "The dialogue from the dark sorcerer is a bit cliché. Try to make his character more menacing and unique."

- **Suggestion:** "Give the sorcerer more distinctive dialogue that reveals his character and intentions."

Revised Excerpt with Feedback Incorporated

Liora stood before the Heart of the Forest, a glowing crystal pulsing with vibrant energy. The air around it hummed with power, resonating deep within her. She felt a profound connection to the crystal, as if it were calling out to her very soul. Her fingers tingled as she reached out, drawn by its magnetic aura.

Suddenly, the dark sorcerer emerged from the shadows, his presence a chilling contrast to the crystal's warmth. His eyes, cold and calculating, fixed hungrily on the Heart of the Forest. "You are a fool to think you can challenge me," he hissed, his voice dripping with malice.

Liora's heart pounded in her chest. She could feel her courage wavering, but she steadied herself, drawing a deep breath. With trembling hands, she raised them before her, willing a shield of light to form. The effort was immense, sweat beading on her forehead as she concentrated. Slowly, a shimmering barrier began to take shape, its light flickering uncertainly.

The sorcerer's lips curled into a cruel smile. "Pathetic," he sneered, and with a swift motion, he hurled a bolt of dark energy towards her. Liora braced herself, barely managing to deflect the attack with her fragile shield. The impact sent a jolt through her body, and she felt her strength waning, the shield flickering dangerously.

Reflection

Before Feedback:

- **Rushed Confrontation:** The original passage quickly moved through the confrontation, missing opportunities to build tension and stakes.
- **Abrupt Actions:** Liora's shield appeared without much effort or struggle, reducing the impact of the moment.
- **Cliché Dialogue:** The dark sorcerer's dialogue was generic and did not add depth to his character.

After Feedback:

- **Enhanced Tension and Stakes:** Added descriptive details about Liora's feelings and the environment to build suspense leading up to the confrontation.
- **Internal Struggle:** Showed Liora's effort and struggle to summon the shield, making her actions more impactful.
- **Distinctive Dialogue:** Revised the dark sorcerer's dialogue to make it more menacing and unique, revealing more about his character and intentions.

Incorporating feedback from beta readers helped to address issues I had overlooked, enhancing the emotional depth and narrative complexity of the scene. This exercise demonstrates the value of external perspectives in refining and improving a manuscript.

7. Ensuring Consistency

Exercise: Consistency Check

- **Task:** Create a checklist of key details in your manuscript, such as character names, settings, timelines, and factual information. Read through your manuscript and ensure these details are consistent throughout.
- **Goal:** To maintain the credibility and coherence of your manuscript by ensuring consistency.

Example

Consistency Checklist

Character Names:

1. Liora
2. The Guardian
3. Dark Sorcerer (actual name: Malakar)
4. Liora's mother: Elara
5. Liora's best friend: Jorin

Settings:

1. Village: Evergreen Hollow
2. Forest: The Enchanted Forest
3. Heart of the Forest: The Glowing Crystal
4. Dark Sorcerer's Lair: The Shadow Keep

Timelines:

1. Liora's age: 17
2. Time since the last guardian: 100 years
3. Duration of Liora's journey: 3 months

Factual Information:

1. The Heart of the Forest is the source of all magic.
2. The Guardian can only appear in times of great need.
3. Malakar's goal is to control the Heart to dominate the realms.
4. The Enchanted Forest is home to various magical creatures, including luminescent plants, talking animals, and ancient trees.

Original Excerpt from Chapter 7: Returning Home

Liora walked back to Evergreen Village, her heart heavy with the weight of her journey. She thought about the Guardian, who had guided her through the Enchanted Woods. The Heart of the Forest had been saved, and the evil sorcerer was defeated. Her friend, Joren, met her at the edge of the village, relief evident in his eyes.

"Liora, you did it!" Joren exclaimed. "The village is safe because of you."

Liora smiled, thinking about how much had changed in the past two months. She was no longer the same girl who had left Evergreen. She was stronger, wiser, and ready to face whatever challenges lay ahead.

Revised Excerpt with Consistency Check

Liora walked back to Evergreen Hollow, her heart heavy with the weight of her journey. She thought about the Guardian, who had guided her through the Enchanted Forest. The Heart of the Forest had been saved, and the dark sorcerer Malakar was defeated. Her friend, Jorin, met her at the edge of the village, relief evident in his eyes.

"Liora, you did it!" Jorin exclaimed. "The village is safe because of you."

Liora smiled, thinking about how much had changed in the past three months. She was no longer the same girl who had left Evergreen Hollow. She was stronger, wiser, and ready to face whatever challenges lay ahead.

Reflection

Before Consistency Check:

- **Character Names:** Incorrect spelling of Jorin as "Joren."
- **Settings:** Referred to "Evergreen Village" instead of "Evergreen Hollow."
- **Timelines:** Incorrectly stated the journey's duration as two months instead of three months.
- **Factual Information:** General information was correct but needed specificity.

After Consistency Check:

- **Corrected Character Names:** Ensured the correct spelling of Jorin.
- **Consistent Settings:** Used the correct name "Evergreen Hollow" consistently.
- **Accurate Timelines:** Corrected the journey duration to three months.
- **Maintained Factual Consistency:** Ensured all details about the journey and characters were accurate.

By creating and using a consistency checklist, I ensured that key details in my manuscript remained consistent throughout the narrative. This exercise helped maintain the credibility and coherence of the story, providing a seamless reading experience for the audience.

8. Fostering Emotional Impact

Exercise: Emotional Intensity Enhancement

- **Task:** Identify key scenes meant to evoke strong emotions. Revisit these scenes and use descriptive language, pacing, and dialogue to heighten the emotional stakes. Read these scenes aloud to gauge their impact.
- **Goal:** To connect with your readers on a deeper level by enhancing the emotional resonance of your manuscript.

Example

Original Excerpt from Chapter 6: The Final Confrontation

Liora faced Malakar, the dark sorcerer, in the heart of the forest. "You will not take the Heart," she said, her voice trembling. Malakar laughed. "You think you can stop me?" he taunted. They fought fiercely, and Liora used all her strength to protect the Heart. In the end, she managed to defeat Malakar, but she was exhausted and fell to the ground, breathing heavily.

Enhanced Excerpt with Emotional Intensity

Liora stood in the heart of the forest, her gaze locked on Malakar, the dark sorcerer. The air crackled with tension, the ancient trees around them whispering in anticipation. Her hands trembled as she gripped her staff, but her voice was steady. "You will not take the Heart," she declared, her eyes burning with determination.

Malakar's lips curled into a sinister smile. "You think you can stop me?" he sneered, his voice dripping with contempt. He raised his hands, dark energy swirling around his fingers, casting an eerie glow on his malevolent face.

Liora's heart pounded in her chest, each beat echoing in her ears like a war drum. She felt the weight of the forest's magic coursing through her veins, a wild and untamed force. Drawing a deep breath, she summoned all her strength, channeling the light within her. A shield of shimmering energy enveloped her, and she stepped forward, ready to face the darkness.

The clash was explosive. Bolts of dark energy collided with her shield, sending shockwaves through the forest. Each attack from Malakar was met with fierce resistance, but the strain was immense. Sweat poured down Liora's face, her muscles ached, and her vision blurred. Yet, she fought on, driven by the resolve to protect the Heart.

Malakar's taunts grew louder, more desperate. "You cannot win, girl!" he shouted, frustration creeping into his voice. But Liora refused to yield. With a final, defiant cry, she unleashed a burst of pure light, piercing through the darkness. Malakar's scream echoed through the trees as he was engulfed by the blinding radiance.

When the light faded, Liora collapsed to her knees, the forest eerily silent around her. She could barely breathe, each gasp a struggle. Her vision swam, but she forced herself to stay conscious, to see the Heart of the Forest still glowing with its gentle, life-giving light. Tears streamed down her face, a mixture of relief and overwhelming exhaustion.

"Is it over?" she whispered, her voice barely audible. The Guardian appeared beside her, placing a comforting hand on her shoulder. "You did well, Liora. The forest is safe, thanks to you."

Liora closed her eyes, allowing herself a moment of peace. She had faced the darkness and emerged victorious, but the cost had been high. As she lay on the forest floor, surrounded by the whispering trees, she knew she had given everything to protect the Heart—and it had been worth it.

Reflection

Before Enhancement:

- **Basic Descriptions:** The original scene had simple descriptions and lacked depth in emotional portrayal.
- **Pacing:** The confrontation felt rushed, with little buildup of tension.
- **Dialogue:** Dialogue was minimal and did not fully convey the characters' emotions.

After Enhancement:

- **Descriptive Language:** Added vivid descriptions of the setting, characters' actions, and their internal states to heighten emotional impact.
- **Pacing:** Slowed down the scene to build suspense and intensity, making each moment more impactful.
- **Dialogue:** Expanded dialogue to reveal more about the characters' emotions and motivations, enhancing the scene's drama.

By revisiting key scenes and using descriptive language, pacing, and dialogue, I enhanced the emotional intensity of the narrative. Reading the scenes aloud helped gauge their impact, ensuring that the emotional stakes connected deeply with the readers. This exercise demonstrates how focusing on emotional resonance can transform pivotal moments in a manuscript.

9. Refining Your Voice

Exercise: Voice Consistency Review

- **Task:** Read through your manuscript and highlight passages where your voice feels strongest and most authentic. Compare these to sections where your voice feels weaker. Revise the weaker sections to align more closely with your authentic voice.
- **Goal:** To ensure your unique voice comes through clearly and consistently throughout your manuscript.

Example

Strong Passage Example

Excerpt from Chapter 3: The Guardian's Revelation

Liora stood at the edge of the clearing, her breath catching in her throat. Before her, the Guardian shimmered like a mirage, its ethereal form pulsating with a soft, otherworldly light. The air around them seemed to hum with ancient power, a silent symphony that spoke of forgotten times and hidden truths. Liora felt a profound connection to this place, as if the very essence of the forest was whispering secrets to her soul.

"You have been chosen, Liora," the Guardian intoned, its voice a harmonious blend of wind and water. "The fate of the Enchanted Forest rests in your hands."

Weak Passage Example

Excerpt from Chapter 6: The Final Confrontation

Liora faced Malakar, the dark sorcerer, in the heart of the forest. "You will not take the Heart," she said, her voice trembling. Malakar laughed. "You think you can stop me?" he taunted. They fought fiercely, and Liora used all her strength to protect the Heart. In the end, she managed to defeat Malakar, but she was exhausted and fell to the ground, breathing heavily.

Revised Passage to Align with Authentic Voice

Liora stood resolute in the heart of the forest, her eyes fixed on Malakar, the dark sorcerer whose presence seemed to suck the light from the surrounding trees. "You will not take the Heart," she declared, her voice steady despite the storm of emotions raging within her.

Malakar's laugh was a cold, sharp sound that echoed through the clearing. "You think you can stop me?" he sneered, dark energy crackling at his fingertips.

The air between them shimmered with tension as they squared off, each moment stretching into eternity. Liora could feel the forest's magic thrumming through her veins, a wild and untamed force. She raised her staff, summoning every ounce of strength and willpower she possessed. A barrier of shimmering light erupted around her, clashing violently with Malakar's dark magic.

The forest seemed to hold its breath as their powers collided, creating a blinding explosion of light and shadow. Sweat dripped down Liora's face as she pushed back against the dark sorcerer's onslaught, her muscles burning with exertion. Each heartbeat echoed in her ears like a drum, urging her to fight on.

"You cannot win!" Malakar shouted, his voice tinged with desperation. But Liora felt a surge of defiance. With a final, desperate cry, she unleashed a torrent of pure light, breaking through the darkness. Malakar's scream was swallowed by the radiant burst, his form disintegrating into shadows.

As the light faded, Liora collapsed to her knees, gasping for breath. The forest was silent, save for the gentle rustle of leaves. She glanced at the Heart of the Forest, still glowing with its gentle, life-giving light, and allowed herself a moment of relief. She had faced the darkness and emerged victorious, but the battle had taken its toll.

Reflection

Before Revision:

- **Weak Voice:** The original passage had a straightforward, somewhat bland narrative style, lacking the rich, descriptive language that characterized the stronger passages.
- **Inconsistent Tone:** The tone was less immersive and did not convey the same depth of emotion and intensity as the stronger passage.
- **Simplistic Dialogue:** The dialogue was brief and did not fully capture the characters' emotions or the high stakes of the scene.

After Revision:

- **Consistent Voice:** The revised passage uses the same rich, descriptive language and immersive tone as the stronger passage, aligning with the authentic voice.
- **Enhanced Emotional Depth:** The scene now has greater emotional resonance, with vivid descriptions and a focus on Liora's internal struggle and determination.
- **Dynamic Dialogue:** The dialogue is more dynamic and expressive, adding to the tension and character development.

By comparing the weaker sections to the passages where my voice felt strongest, I was able to revise the weaker sections to align more closely with my authentic voice. This exercise helped ensure that my unique voice came through clearly and consistently throughout the manuscript, enhancing the overall impact and coherence of the story.

10. Preparing for Publication

Exercise: Final Polish and Review

- **Task:** After completing all other revisions, read through your manuscript one final time. Focus on any remaining issues, no matter how minor. Ensure the formatting is consistent, and the manuscript is free of errors.
- **Goal:** To present a polished manuscript that demonstrates your commitment to quality and professionalism.

Example

Excerpt from Chapter 7: Returning Home

Before Final Polish

Liora walked back to Evergreen Hollow, her heart heavy with the weight of her journey. She thought about the Guardian, who had guided her through the Enchanted Forest. The Heart of the Forest had been saved, and the dark sorcerer Malakar was defeated. Her friend, Jorin, met her at the edge of the village, relief evident in his eyes.

"Liora, you did it!" Jorin exclaimed. "The village is safe because of you."

Liora smiled, thinking about how much had changed in the past three months. She was no longer the same girl who had left Evergreen Hollow. She was stronger, wiser, and ready to face whatever challenges lay ahead.

Final Polish and Review

Grammar and Punctuation:

- ✓ Check for proper use of commas, periods, and other punctuation marks.
- ✓ Ensure all dialogue punctuation is correct.
- ✓ Verify that there are no grammatical errors.

Formatting:

- ✓ Ensure consistent use of font and size.
- ✓ Check for proper indentation and alignment of paragraphs.
- ✓ Verify that chapter headings are uniformly formatted.

Consistency:

- ✓ Confirm that character names, settings, and timelines are consistent throughout.
- ✓ Ensure the tone and voice are consistent with the rest of the manuscript.

Flow and Readability:

- ✓ Read the passage aloud to check for awkward phrasing.
- ✓ Adjust sentence structure for better flow and readability.
- ✓ Ensure each sentence contributes meaningfully to the narrative.

Polished Excerpt from Chapter 7: Returning Home

Liora walked back to Evergreen Hollow, her heart heavy with the weight of her journey. She thought about the Guardian, who had guided her through the Enchanted Forest. The Heart of the Forest had been saved, and the dark sorcerer Malakar was defeated. Her friend, Jorin, met her at the edge of the village, relief evident in his eyes.

"Liora, you did it!" Jorin exclaimed. "The village is safe because of you."

Liora smiled, reflecting on how much had changed in the past three months. She was no longer the same girl who had left Evergreen Hollow. She was stronger, wiser, and ready to face whatever challenges lay ahead.

Checklist for Final Polish and Review

Grammar and Punctuation:

1. Checked for proper use of commas, periods, and other punctuation marks.
2. Ensured all dialogue punctuation is correct.
3. Verified that there are no grammatical errors.

Formatting:

1. Ensured consistent use of font and size (e.g., Times New Roman, 12pt).
2. Checked for proper indentation and alignment of paragraphs.
3. Verified that chapter headings are uniformly formatted.

Consistency:

1. Confirmed that character names, settings, and timelines are consistent throughout.
2. Ensured the tone and voice are consistent with the rest of the manuscript.

Flow and Readability:

1. Read the passage aloud to check for awkward phrasing.
2. Adjusted sentence structure for better flow and readability.
3. Ensured each sentence contributes meaningfully to the narrative.

Reflection

Before Final Polish:

- **Minor Errors:** There were small issues with grammar and punctuation that needed correction.
- **Formatting Inconsistencies:** Formatting was not uniform throughout the manuscript.
- **Flow and Readability:** Some sentences were slightly awkward, affecting the overall flow.

After Final Polish:

- **Error-Free:** The manuscript is free of grammatical and punctuation errors.
- **Consistent Formatting:** Formatting is consistent, enhancing the professional presentation of the manuscript.
- **Smooth Flow:** Sentence structure and readability have been improved, ensuring a smooth and engaging reading experience.

By conducting a final polish and review, I ensured that my manuscript was polished and ready for publication. This exercise highlights the importance of attention to detail and a commitment to quality, which are essential for presenting a professional and compelling manuscript to readers and publishers.

Reflection and Tips for the Editing and Revising Process

Take a Break

Exercise: Manuscript Rest Period

- **Task:** After completing your first draft, set your manuscript aside for a week or two. Engage in other activities or work on a different project.
- **Goal:** To return to your manuscript with fresh eyes and a more objective perspective.

Edit in Stages

Exercise: Staged Editing Plan

- **Task:** Break the editing process into stages. Start with big-picture elements like structure and plot, then move on to finer details like grammar and style. Create a timeline for each stage.
- **Goal:** To systematically address different aspects of your manuscript, ensuring thorough and effective editing.

Use Tools Wisely

Exercise: Grammar and Style Tools

- **Task:** Utilize grammar-checking tools and style guides to review your manuscript. Perform a manual review after using these tools to catch subtleties and nuances they might miss.
- **Goal:** To enhance the accuracy and polish of your manuscript while relying on your judgment for final revisions.

Read Aloud

Exercise: Read-Aloud Sessions

- **Task:** Read sections of your manuscript aloud, focusing on different aspects such as pacing, rhythm, and clarity. Make notes of any awkward phrasing or errors.
- **Goal:** To catch issues you might overlook when reading silently and to ensure your prose flows naturally.

Stay Open to Feedback

Exercise: Feedback Integration

- **Task:** Regularly share your manuscript with others and seek their feedback. Embrace their constructive criticism and be willing to make changes that improve your work.
- **Goal:** To continuously improve your manuscript based on diverse perspectives and insights.

By embracing these exercises and strategies, you can elevate your manuscript through effective editing and revising. Each round of editing brings you closer to a polished and compelling piece of work that resonates with readers and showcases your artistry as a writer.

Exercises for Chapter 2: Explore Self-Publishing vs. Traditional or Hybrid Publishing

1. Understanding Your Options

Exercise: Research and Compare

- **Task:** Conduct research on self-publishing, traditional publishing, and hybrid publishing. Create a comparison chart that outlines the key differences in terms of process, cost, time, and control.
- **Goal:** To gain a clear understanding of the distinct characteristics and requirements of each publishing route.

Example Comparison Chart:

Aspect	Self-Publishing	Traditional Publishing	Hybrid Publishing
Process	Author handles all aspects	Publisher handles most aspects	Combination of author and publisher tasks
Cost	Upfront costs for editing, design, etc.	Minimal upfront costs, publisher invests	Shared costs, varies by agreement
Time	Quick publication timelines	Longer timelines due to submission process	Moderate timelines
Control	Full creative control	Publisher has significant control	Shared control
Royalties	Higher royalties	Lower royalties, advance payment	Moderate royalties

2. Pros and Cons

Exercise: Pros and Cons List

- **Task:** Write a detailed list of pros and cons for self-publishing, traditional publishing, and hybrid publishing. Consider aspects such as creative control, financial investment, time commitment, and market reach.
- **Goal:** To critically evaluate the benefits and drawbacks of each publishing method.

Example Pros and Cons List:

Self-Publishing:

-
    Pros:

    -
        - Complete creative control
        - Higher royalty rates
        - Faster publication timeline
        - Flexibility in marketing and promotion
    -

    Cons:

    -
        - Upfront costs for editing, design, and marketing
        - Time-consuming for the author
        - Limited access to traditional distribution channels
        - Requires extensive self-promotion

Traditional Publishing:

-

Pros:

-
    - Publisher covers most costs
    - Professional editorial and marketing support
    - Wider distribution network
    - Potential for advance payments
-

Cons:

-
    - Lengthy submission and publication process
    - Less creative control
    - Lower royalty rates
    - Competitive and difficult to break into

Hybrid Publishing:

-

Pros:

-
    - Shared control and responsibilities
    - Professional support with some creative freedom
    - More flexible contracts
    - Combination of both worlds
-

Cons:

-
  - Shared costs, which can be substantial
  - Potential for conflicts in decision-making
  - Varied quality of hybrid publishers
  - Not as well-established or recognized as traditional publishers

---

3. Case Studies

Exercise: Analyze Success Stories

- **Task:** Find and analyze at least two case studies of authors who have succeeded in self-publishing, traditional publishing, and hybrid publishing. Summarize their experiences, challenges, and the outcomes of their chosen publishing paths.
- **Goal:** To learn from real-life examples and understand how different publishing routes can lead to success.

Example Case Studies:

Self-Publishing:

- **Author:** Amanda Hocking
- **Experience:** Initially faced rejection from traditional publishers, decided to self-publish her paranormal romance novels on Amazon Kindle. Achieved significant success and later signed a traditional publishing deal.
- **Outcome:** Sold over a million copies of her self-published books and gained a large fan base, leading to lucrative traditional publishing contracts.

Traditional Publishing:

- **Author:** J.K. Rowling

- **Experience:** Submitted her manuscript for "Harry Potter and the Philosopher's Stone" to multiple publishers before being accepted by Bloomsbury. The publisher provided extensive editorial and marketing support.
- **Outcome:** Achieved global success, with the Harry Potter series becoming one of the best-selling book series of all time, and Rowling becoming one of the wealthiest authors in history.

Hybrid Publishing:

- **Author:** Guy Kawasaki
- **Experience:** Used hybrid publishing for his book "APE: Author, Publisher, Entrepreneur." Partnered with a hybrid publisher to handle aspects like distribution and marketing while maintaining control over the content.
- **Outcome:** Successfully published and marketed his book, benefiting from both professional support and creative control, leading to strong sales and positive reviews.

4. Making the Decision

Exercise: Decision Matrix

- **Task:** Create a decision matrix to help you choose the best publishing path for your book. List your personal and career goals, then rate how well each publishing option meets these goals. Consider factors like control, cost, time, support, and reach.
- **Goal:** To make an informed decision on the best publishing path for your specific needs and objectives.

Example Decision Matrix:

Goal	Self-Publishing	Traditional Publishing	Hybrid Publishing
Creative Control	5	2	4
Upfront Cost	2	4	3

Goal	Self-Publishing	Traditional Publishing	Hybrid Publishing
Time to Publish	5	2	4
Marketing Support	2	5	3
Distribution Reach	3	5	4
Professional Editing	3	5	4
Potential for Royalties	5	3	4
Advance Payment	1	5	3
Flexibility	5	2	4

Scoring:

- 5 = Excellent
- 4 = Good
- 3 = Average
- 2 = Below Average
- 1 = Poor

Example Calculation:

- **Self-Publishing:** (5+2+5+2+3+3+5+1+5) = 31
- **Traditional Publishing:** (2+4+2+5+5+5+3+5+2) = 33
- **Hybrid Publishing:** (4+3+4+3+4+4+4+3+4) = 33

Based on your scores, determine which publishing path aligns best with your goals.

These exercises will help you thoroughly explore and understand the different publishing options available, weigh their pros and cons, learn from real-life examples, and make an informed decision that aligns with your book and career goals.

High Upfront Costs: Vanity presses charge authors sign

Exercises for Chapter 3: Book Marketing

1. Identifying Your Target Audience

Exercise: Create Reader Personas

Task: Develop detailed reader personas for your book. Use market research tools like surveys, social media analytics, and online forums to gather insights about your potential readers. Consider factors such as age, gender, interests, reading preferences, and buying behaviors.

Goal: To create a clear profile of your ideal reader, which will guide your marketing efforts.

Example:

Reader Persona 1:

- **Name:** Sarah Thompson
- **Age:** 34
- **Gender:** Female
- **Interests:** Fantasy novels, mythology, and folklore
- **Reading Preferences:** Enjoys character-driven stories with strong female leads
- **Buying Behaviors:** Frequently purchases books online and reads reviews before buying

Reader Persona 2:

- **Name:** John Miller
- **Age:** 45
- **Gender:** Male
- **Interests:** Historical fiction, war novels, and biographies
- **Reading Preferences:** Prefers detailed historical contexts and realistic character development
- **Buying Behaviors:** Buys books both online and in-store, follows recommendations from book clubs and forums

---

2. Creating a Marketing Plan

Exercise: Develop a Marketing Plan Template

Task: Create a template for your marketing plan that includes goals, strategies, tactics, and metrics. Use this template to outline your book marketing efforts.

Goal: To have a structured roadmap for your marketing activities that ensures you stay on track and measure your success.

Example Template:

Goals:

- Increase book sales by 20% in the first quarter after launch
- Grow email list by 500 subscribers within six months
- Enhance social media presence with a 30% increase in engagement

Strategies:

- Online advertising
- Content marketing
- Book tours and signings

Tactics:

- Facebook and Instagram ads
- Weekly blog posts on book-related themes
- Schedule book signings at local bookstores

Metrics:

- Sales numbers from various platforms
- Website traffic and email sign-ups
- Social media engagement rates (likes, shares, comments)

---

3. Building an Author Platform

Exercise: Design Your Author Website

Task: Outline the structure and content for your author website. Ensure it includes an author bio, book information, a blog, and a contact page. Plan regular updates to keep the site fresh and engaging.

Goal: To establish a professional and user-friendly online presence that serves as the hub of your marketing efforts.

Example Outline:

Homepage:

- Welcome message
- Latest book release with a purchase link

About Page:

- Detailed author bio
- Photos and fun facts

Books Page:

- Information about each book (synopsis, reviews, purchase links)
- Upcoming releases

Blog:

- Regular posts on writing tips, book themes, and personal insights

Contact Page:

- Email form for reader inquiries
- Links to social media profiles

4. Content Marketing

Exercise: Create a Content Calendar

Task: Develop a content calendar for your blog, social media posts, and other content marketing efforts. Plan topics, dates, and formats (articles, videos, podcasts).

Goal: To ensure consistent, high-quality content that engages your audience and builds your authority as an author.

Example Content Calendar:

Date	Content Type	Topic	Platform
Jan 5	Blog Post	Writing Strong Female Characters	Author Blog
Jan 12	Video	Behind the Scenes of My Writing	YouTube
Jan	Guest Blog	Historical Accuracy in	Partner

Date	Content Type	Topic	Platform
19		Fiction	Blog
Jan 26	Podcast	Interview with a Fellow Author	Spotify

5. Leveraging Book Reviews and Testimonials

Exercise: Plan a Review Campaign

Task: Develop a campaign to solicit book reviews. Identify book bloggers, influencers, and loyal readers to receive Advance Review Copies (ARCs). Create a follow-up plan to encourage reviews on Amazon, Goodreads, and social media.

Goal: To gather positive reviews and testimonials that build credibility and attract new readers.

Example Campaign Plan:

    Identify Targets:

- List of 20 book bloggers
- 10 influencers in your genre
- Top 50 loyal readers from your email list

    Send ARCs:

- Prepare and send personalized emails offering ARCs
- Include a request for an honest review

    Follow-Up:

- Send a reminder email two weeks after sending ARCs

- Provide direct links to review pages

Showcase Reviews:

- Highlight the best reviews on your website and social media
- Use quotes in marketing materials

---

6. Paid Advertising

Exercise: Develop an Advertising Strategy

Task: Create an advertising strategy for your book, detailing your budget, target platforms, and ad formats. Plan and execute ads on social media, search engines, and book promotion sites.

Goal: To increase your book's visibility and reach a broader audience through targeted advertising.

Example Advertising Strategy:

Budget:

- Total Budget: $500/month

Platforms:

- Facebook Ads: $200
- Instagram Ads: $150
- Google Ads: $100
- BookBub Promotions: $50

Ad Formats:

- **Facebook/Instagram:** Carousel ads showcasing book cover, key quotes, and purchase link
- **Google Ads:** Text ads targeting keywords related to your book's genre
- **BookBub:** Featured deal ad for a limited-time discount

Execution Plan:

- Design ad creatives
- Set up targeting parameters
- Monitor ad performance weekly and adjust as needed

7. Measuring and Adjusting Your Strategy

Exercise: Create a Performance Dashboard

Task: Set up a dashboard to track your key performance indicators (KPIs) such as sales numbers, website traffic, email open rates, and social media engagement. Use tools like Google Analytics, social media insights, and email marketing analytics.

Goal: To regularly review your marketing performance and make data-driven adjustments to your strategies.

Example Performance Dashboard:

Metrics to Track:

- **Sales Numbers:** Daily, weekly, and monthly sales from all platforms
- **Website Traffic:** Page views, unique visitors, bounce rate
- **Email Open Rates:** Percentage of opened emails, click-through rates
- **Social Media Engagement:** Likes, shares, comments, follower growth

Tools:

- Google Analytics for website metrics
- Social media platform insights (Facebook, Instagram, Twitter)
- Email marketing software analytics (Mailchimp, ConvertKit)

Review Schedule:

- Weekly review of all metrics
- Monthly deep-dive analysis to identify trends and areas for improvement
- Quarterly strategic adjustment based on performance data

By completing these exercises, you will develop a comprehensive understanding of book marketing, enabling you to create effective strategies and tactics to promote your book. This will help you build a successful author career by reaching and engaging your target audience, driving sales, and establishing your brand.

1. Book Tours (Virtual and In-Person)

Exercise: Plan a Virtual Book Tour

Task: Create a detailed plan for a virtual book tour, including blog stops, webinars, live streams, and podcast appearances. Identify potential partners and schedule dates for each event.

Goal: To reach a global audience through cost-effective online engagements.

Example Plan:

Blog Stops:

- Partner with 10 book bloggers for interviews, guest posts, reviews, and giveaways.
- Schedule: One blog stop per week for 10 weeks.

Webinars and Live Streams:

- Host a live webinar on Zoom to discuss your book and engage with readers.
- Schedule: Two webinars—one at launch and another two months later.

Podcasts:

- Appear on 5 podcasts that cater to your target audience.
- Schedule: One podcast appearance every two weeks.

---

2. Launch Parties

Exercise: Organize a Virtual Launch Party

Task: Plan a virtual book launch party on a platform like Zoom or Facebook Live. Outline the agenda, including readings, Q&A sessions, and interactive elements like contests and giveaways.

Goal: To generate excitement and buzz around your book's release, reaching a broader audience online.

Example Agenda:

- **Welcome and Introduction:** Brief introduction about yourself and your book.
- **Live Reading:** Read a captivating excerpt from your book.
- **Q&A Session:** Answer questions from the audience.

- **Contests and Giveaways:** Run a live contest or giveaway, encouraging engagement.
- **Closing Remarks:** Thank attendees and provide links to purchase your book.

---

3. Giveaways and Contests

Exercise: Plan a Social Media Giveaway

Task: Design a social media giveaway campaign for Instagram. Determine the rules, duration, and prize. Create engaging posts to promote the giveaway.

Goal: To increase engagement, reach new readers, and generate buzz for your book.

Example Campaign:

Rules:

- Follow your Instagram account.
- Like and share the giveaway post.
- Tag three friends in the comments.

Duration:

- One week.

Prize:

- Signed copy of your book and a $25 Amazon gift card.

Promotion Posts:

- **Day 1:** Announce the giveaway with a captivating image and clear instructions.

- **Day 3:** Reminder post with a teaser about your book.
- **Day 6:** Final call to participate in the giveaway.

---

4. Speaking Engagements and Signings

Exercise: Schedule Library Talks

Task: Contact local libraries to offer talks about your book and the writing process. Prepare a presentation outline and promotional materials.

Goal: To connect with local readers and promote your book through personal interaction.

Example Presentation Outline:

1. **Introduction:** Briefly introduce yourself and your book.
2. **Writing Process:** Share insights into your writing journey and process.
3. **Book Reading:** Read an excerpt from your book.
4. **Interactive Q&A:** Engage with the audience by answering their questions.
5. **Book Signing:** Offer signed copies of your book.

Promotional Materials:

- Flyers and posters for the library to display.
- Social media posts to promote the event.

---

5. Special Discount Campaigns

Exercise: Plan an Ebook Discount Campaign

Task: Design a limited-time discount campaign for your ebook on Amazon KDP Select. Determine the discount, promotion duration, and marketing tactics.

Goal: To attract new readers and boost sales through a strategic discount offer.

Example Campaign Plan:

Discount:

- 50% off the regular price.

Duration:

- One week.

Marketing Tactics:

- **Email Newsletter:** Announce the discount to your email subscribers.
- **Social Media Posts:** Promote the discount on all social media platforms.
- **Book Promotion Sites:** List the discount on book promotion sites like BookBub.

---

6. Utilizing Email Marketing

Exercise: Develop an Email Newsletter Series

Task: Create a series of email newsletters to keep your subscribers engaged and informed about your book. Plan the content for each email and the schedule.

Goal: To maintain regular communication with your readers and promote your book effectively.

Example Newsletter Series:

1. **Welcome Email:** Introduction and thank you for subscribing.
2. **Book Teaser:** Share the first chapter or an exclusive excerpt.
3. **Behind-the-Scenes:** Insights into your writing process and inspiration.
4. **Launch Announcement:** Details about the book release and how to purchase.
5. **Exclusive Offers:** Special discounts or bonus content for subscribers.
6. **Review Request:** Encourage readers to leave reviews and share feedback.

---

7. Engaging with Influencers and Bloggers

Exercise: Plan a Blogger Outreach Campaign

Task: Identify 10 book bloggers and influencers in your genre. Reach out to them with personalized messages offering a free copy of your book in exchange for a review or feature.

Goal: To leverage the influence of bloggers and reach a wider audience.

Example Outreach Plan:

Step 1: Research and List Influencers

- Compile a list of 10 influencers with a strong following in your genre.

Step 2: Craft Personalized Messages

- Write a personalized message for each influencer, highlighting why your book would interest their audience.

Step 3: Send ARCs

- Offer to send a free Advance Review Copy (ARC) of your book.

Step 4: Follow-Up

- Send a follow-up email a week after the initial contact to confirm receipt and offer additional information.

---

8. Leveraging Paid Advertising

Exercise: Create a Facebook Ad Campaign

Task: Design a targeted Facebook ad campaign for your book. Define your budget, target audience, ad creatives, and schedule.

Goal: To increase your book's visibility and attract potential readers through targeted advertising.

Example Campaign Plan:

Budget:

- $200 over two weeks.

Target Audience:

- Age: 25-45
- Interests: Reading, specific genres related to your book
- Locations: Major English-speaking countries

Ad Creatives:

- **Ad Image:** High-quality book cover image.
- **Ad Copy:** Engaging and concise text highlighting the book's unique selling points.
- **Call-to-Action:** "Buy Now" button linking to the purchase page.

Schedule:

- Run ads for two weeks, monitoring performance daily and making adjustments as needed.

By completing these exercises, you will develop a comprehensive set of promotion strategies to effectively boost your book's visibility and drive sales. These targeted activities will help you engage with your audience, create buzz, and establish a strong foundation for your book's success.

Building a Brand: Creating an Author Brand that Resonates with Your Target Audience

Understanding Your Author Brand

Your author brand is the unique combination of your voice, style, and persona that distinguishes you from other authors. It's how readers perceive you and your work. A strong, consistent brand helps attract and retain readers, making your marketing efforts more effective.

Exercises for Building an Author Brand

1. Defining Your Brand Identity

Exercise: Brand Identity Worksheet

Task: Complete a brand identity worksheet to clarify your author brand. Consider your writing style, themes, personality, and the message you want to convey.

Goal: To create a clear and cohesive brand identity that resonates with your target audience.

Example Worksheet:

Writing Style:

- Describe your writing style (e.g., lyrical, straightforward, humorous).
- Identify the common themes in your books (e.g., adventure, romance, self-discovery).

Personality:

- List adjectives that describe your personality (e.g., witty, thoughtful, adventurous).
- Think about how you want readers to perceive you (e.g., approachable, inspiring).

Message:

- Define the core message or values you want to communicate through your work (e.g., empowerment, resilience, love).

---

2. Creating a Visual Identity

Exercise: Design Your Author Logo and Color Scheme

Task: Create a logo and select a color scheme that reflects your brand identity. Use design tools or work with a graphic designer to develop these elements.

Goal: To establish a visual identity that complements your written brand and is easily recognizable.

Example Plan:

Logo:

- Design a logo that incorporates elements related to your writing style or themes. For example, if you write fantasy, your logo could include mystical symbols.

Color Scheme:

- Choose a color scheme that evokes the emotions and tone of your books. For example, soft pastels for romance novels or bold, dark colors for thrillers.

---

3. Developing Your Online Presence

Exercise: Optimize Your Social Media Profiles

Task: Review and update your social media profiles to reflect your brand identity. Ensure consistency across platforms in terms of imagery, bio, and content.

Goal: To create a cohesive online presence that reinforces your author brand and engages your target audience.

Example Checklist:

Profile Picture:

- Use a professional photo that reflects your brand's personality.

Cover Image:

- Choose a cover image that highlights your latest book or reflects your brand's visual identity.

Bio:

- Write a bio that encapsulates your writing style, themes, and personality. Include a call-to-action for readers to follow or engage with you.

Content:

- Post content that aligns with your brand values and engages your audience (e.g., behind-the-scenes looks at your writing process, quotes from your books, personal reflections).

---

4. Crafting Your Author Bio

Exercise: Write a Compelling Author Bio

Task: Write and refine your author bio for different platforms (website, social media, book jackets). Tailor each version to fit the platform while maintaining a consistent voice and message.

Goal: To introduce yourself to readers in a way that aligns with your brand and piques their interest in your work.

Example Author Bio:

Website Bio:

- Long version: "Jane Doe is a fantasy author who weaves tales of magic and adventure. With a penchant for creating intricate worlds and compelling characters, Jane invites readers to escape reality and embark on unforgettable journeys. When she's not writing, Jane enjoys exploring forests and ancient ruins, always on the lookout for the next story idea. Her debut novel, 'Enchanted Realms,' has captivated readers and critics alike, earning her a spot on the bestseller list. Connect with Jane on social media for updates on her latest projects and musings on all things fantasy."

Social Media Bio:

- Short version: "Fantasy author. Creator of magical worlds and epic adventures. Follow for updates on my latest books and writing tips. ✨ #FantasyWriter"

---

5. Engaging with Your Audience

Exercise: Plan Interactive Content

Task: Develop a content plan that includes interactive elements such as Q&A sessions, live readings, and polls. Schedule these activities regularly to engage with your audience.

Goal: To foster a strong connection with your readers and build a loyal community around your brand.

Example Content Plan:

Monthly Q&A Sessions:

- Host live Q&A sessions on Instagram or Facebook where readers can ask questions about your books, writing process, or personal interests.

Live Readings:

- Schedule live readings of your book excerpts on YouTube or Facebook Live, followed by a discussion with viewers.

Polls and Surveys:

- Use Twitter or Instagram Stories to create polls and surveys about upcoming projects, book cover designs, or character names to involve readers in the creative process.

6. Networking with Other Authors

Exercise: Join Author Networks and Collaborate

Task: Identify and join author networks, writing groups, and professional associations. Look for opportunities to collaborate with other authors on joint projects, cross-promotions, or anthologies.

Goal: To expand your reach, share resources, and build relationships within the writing community.

Example Collaboration Ideas:

Joint Projects:

- Collaborate on an anthology with authors in your genre, contributing short stories that align with a common theme.

Cross-Promotions:

- Partner with other authors for cross-promotional campaigns, such as featuring each other's books in newsletters or social media shoutouts.

Guest Blogging:

- Write guest posts for each other's blogs, sharing insights on writing, publishing, or book promotion.

---

7. Consistency in Branding

Exercise: Develop a Brand Style Guide

Task: Create a brand style guide that outlines your visual and written branding elements. Include guidelines for logo usage, color schemes, fonts, tone of voice, and key messaging.

Goal: To ensure consistency across all your marketing materials and platforms, reinforcing your brand identity.

Example Brand Style Guide:

Logo Usage:

- Provide different versions of your logo (color, black and white, transparent background) and specify when and how each version should be used.

Color Scheme:

- List the primary and secondary colors of your brand, including HEX, RGB, and CMYK values.

Fonts:

- Choose fonts for headings, body text, and any special text elements. Specify when and where each font should be used.

Tone of Voice:

- Define the tone of voice for your communications (e.g., friendly, authoritative, whimsical) and provide examples of key phrases and language to use.

Key Messaging:

- Outline the core messages you want to convey in your marketing materials, ensuring they align with your brand values and goals.

By completing these exercises, you will build a strong, consistent author brand that resonates with your target audience. This foundation will enhance your marketing efforts, helping you attract and retain readers while establishing your unique identity in the literary world.

1. Choosing the Right Platforms

Exercise: Platform Selection and Analysis

Task: Evaluate different social media platforms to determine which ones best align with your target audience and content. Create a profile on each selected platform and outline your goals for each.

Goal: To identify the most effective platforms for promoting your book and engaging with your audience.

Example Analysis:

Facebook:

- **Target Audience:** Adults aged 30-60
- **Goals:** Build a community, host virtual events, share diverse content
- **Content Types:** Blog posts, event announcements, interactive polls

Twitter:

- **Target Audience:** Adults aged 25-45
- **Goals:** Engage in real-time conversations, network with authors, share updates
- **Content Types:** Short updates, industry news, hashtags for visibility

Instagram:

- **Target Audience:** Young adults aged 18-35
- **Goals:** Showcase visuals, share book aesthetics, engage with creative content
- **Content Types:** Book covers, quotes, behind-the-scenes, Stories, Reels

2. Creating Engaging Content

Exercise: Content Creation Challenge

Task: Plan and create different types of content for your social media platforms. Aim to produce at least one piece of content for each category: behind-the-scenes, teasers/excerpts, visuals, interactive content, live sessions, and user-generated content.

Goal: To diversify your content and increase engagement with your audience.

Example Content Plan:

Behind-the-Scenes:

- Share a photo of your writing desk with a caption about your current writing process.

Teasers and Excerpts:

- Post a gripping excerpt from your book with an eye-catching image.

Visuals:

- Create a quote graphic using Canva and share it on Instagram.

Interactive Content:

- Host a poll on Twitter asking readers which character they like best.

Live Sessions:

- Schedule a live Q&A session on Facebook to interact with readers.

User-Generated Content:

- Encourage readers to share photos of themselves with your book and repost the best ones.

---

3. Building a Content Calendar

Exercise: Develop a Monthly Content Calendar

Task: Create a monthly content calendar that includes the types of content you will post each day, the platforms you will use, and the specific goals for each post.

Goal: To ensure consistent and varied content that aligns with your marketing goals.

Example Content Calendar:

Date	Platform	Content Type	Description
1st Monday	Facebook	Blog Post	Share a new blog post about your writing process
1st Tuesday	Twitter	Poll	Ask followers about their favorite book genres
1st Wednesday	Instagram	Visual Quote	Post a quote graphic from your book
1st Thursday	Facebook	Behind-the-Scenes	Share a photo of your writing desk
1st Friday	Instagram	Teaser/Excerpt	Share an excerpt from your book

Date	Platform	Content Type	Description
1st Saturday	Twitter	Industry News	Tweet about recent news in the book industry
1st Sunday	Facebook	Live Session	Host a live Q&A session with readers

4. Engaging with Your Audience

Exercise: Daily Engagement Routine

Task: Establish a daily routine for engaging with your audience on social media. This includes responding to comments, participating in discussions, and showcasing reader contributions.

Goal: To build strong relationships and foster a sense of community among your readers.

Example Daily Routine:

- **Morning:** Spend 15 minutes responding to comments on your latest posts.
- **Afternoon:** Participate in relevant Twitter conversations using industry hashtags.
- **Evening:** Share a reader's photo or review on Instagram Stories.

5. Leveraging Paid Advertising

Exercise: Design and Implement a Facebook Ad Campaign

Task: Create a Facebook ad campaign to promote your book. Define your budget, target audience, and ad creatives. Implement the campaign and monitor its performance.

Goal: To increase your book's visibility and attract new readers through targeted advertising.

Example Campaign Plan:

Budget:

- $100 over two weeks.

Target Audience:

- Age: 25-45
- Interests: Reading, specific book genres
- Location: English-speaking countries

Ad Creatives:

- **Image Ad:** High-quality image of your book cover.
- **Video Ad:** Short video trailer for your book.
- **Carousel Ad:** Multiple images showcasing different aspects of your book.

Schedule:

- Run ads continuously for two weeks, adjusting based on performance metrics.

---

6. Building and Nurturing an Email List

Exercise: Create an Email Lead Magnet

Task: Develop a valuable lead magnet to encourage email sign-ups. Promote this lead magnet on your website and social media.

Goal: To grow your email list and maintain direct communication with your readers.

Example Lead Magnet:

Offer:

- Free downloadable short story related to your book.

Promotion:

- **Website:** Pop-up form offering the free short story in exchange for email sign-up.
- **Social Media:** Posts highlighting the free offer with a call-to-action to sign up.

---

7. Collaborating with Influencers and Bloggers

Exercise: Influencer Outreach Plan

Task: Identify and reach out to 10 influencers and bloggers relevant to your genre. Offer them a free copy of your book in exchange for a review or feature.

Goal: To expand your reach and gain credibility through influencer endorsements.

Example Outreach Plan:

Step 1: Research and List Influencers

- Compile a list of 10 influencers with a strong following in your genre.

Step 2: Craft Personalized Messages

- Write a personalized message for each influencer, highlighting why your book would interest their audience.

Step 3: Send ARCs

- Offer to send a free Advance Review Copy (ARC) of your book.

Step 4: Follow-Up

- Send a follow-up email a week after the initial contact to confirm receipt and offer additional information.

---

8. Utilizing Analytics and Adjusting Strategies

Exercise: Analytics Review and Strategy Adjustment

Task: Use analytics tools to review the performance of your social media and digital marketing efforts. Identify what works and what doesn't, and adjust your strategy accordingly.

Goal: To continuously improve your marketing efforts based on data-driven insights.

Example Analytics Review:

Tools:

- Google Analytics for website traffic
- Facebook Insights for engagement metrics
- Twitter Analytics for tweet performance
- Instagram Insights for follower growth and post engagement

Review Metrics:

- Website Traffic: Page views, unique visitors, bounce rate
- Social Media Engagement: Likes, shares, comments, retweets
- Email Marketing: Open rates, click-through rates, conversion rates

Strategy Adjustment:

- Focus more on content types that show higher engagement.
- Adjust posting times based on when your audience is most active.
- Experiment with new content formats or platforms based on performance data.

By completing these exercises, you will effectively leverage social media and digital marketing to promote your book and engage with your audience. This comprehensive approach will help you build a strong online presence, drive book sales, and foster a loyal community around your work.

Exercises for Effective Public Relations (PR)

1. Crafting a Compelling Press Kit

Exercise: Create Your Press Kit

Task: Develop a comprehensive press kit that includes an author bio, book synopsis, press release, high-quality images, and contact information. Use this kit to approach media outlets and bloggers.

Goal: To have a ready-to-use press kit that captures the attention of journalists and media representatives.

Example Press Kit Components:

Author Bio:

- A 150-word biography that highlights your background, achievements, and expertise. Tailor it to reflect your personality and the themes of your book.

Book Synopsis:

- A 200-word captivating summary of your book that highlights the main plot points, unique aspects, and why readers will find it compelling.

Press Release:

- A professional press release announcing your book's launch, including the release date, a brief overview, and any relevant accolades or endorsements.

High-Quality Images:

- High-resolution images of your book cover, author photo, and any other relevant visuals.

Contact Information:

- An email address, phone number, and links to your social media profiles.

---

2. Writing and Distributing Press Releases

Exercise: Write a Press Release

Task: Craft a press release for your book's launch. Follow the structure of a compelling headline, strong opening paragraph, detailed body, and clear call to action. Distribute the press release using PR services and direct outreach.

Goal: To generate media coverage and create buzz around your book.

Example Press Release Structure:

Headline:

- "New Fantasy Novel 'Enchanted Realms' by Jane Doe Set to Captivate Readers This Spring"

Opening Paragraph:

- "Acclaimed author Jane Doe announces the release of her highly anticipated fantasy novel, 'Enchanted Realms,' set to hit bookstores on April 15th, 2024. This captivating tale of magic, adventure, and self-discovery is poised to become a must-read for fantasy enthusiasts."

Body:

- Provide more detailed information about your book, including unique selling points, background information, and relevant quotes or testimonials.

Call to Action:

- "For more information, visit [Your Website]. To request a review copy or schedule an interview, please contact [Your Contact Information]."

Distribution:

- Use PR distribution services like PR Newswire, Business Wire, and direct outreach to journalists, bloggers, and media outlets.

---

3. Securing Media Coverage

Exercise: Media Outreach Plan

Task: Identify relevant media outlets, blogs, podcasts, and influencers. Create personalized pitches for each, highlighting why your book is relevant to their audience and offering unique angles or story ideas. Follow up with a polite reminder if you haven't received a response.

Goal: To secure media coverage and increase your book's visibility.

Example Media Outreach Plan:

Step 1: Identify Media Outlets

- Research and list 20 relevant media outlets, blogs, podcasts, and influencers.

Step 2: Craft Personalized Pitches

- Write personalized pitches for each outlet, emphasizing the unique aspects of your book and why it would interest their audience.

Step 3: Send Review Copies

- Offer free review copies of your book to journalists and bloggers.

Step 4: Follow-Up

- Send a follow-up email a week after the initial contact to confirm receipt and offer additional information.

---

4. Participating in Interviews and Features

Exercise: Interview Preparation

Task: Prepare for interviews by identifying your key messages, practicing your delivery, and rehearsing answers to common questions. Schedule practice sessions with a friend or in front of a mirror.

Goal: To deliver confident and engaging interviews that effectively promote your book.

Example Interview Preparation:

Key Messages:

- Highlight the unique aspects of your book, your writing process, and your personal journey.

Practice Answers:

- Prepare answers to common questions such as "What inspired you to write this book?" and "What message do you hope readers take away?"

Engaging and Authentic Delivery:

- Practice speaking concisely and confidently, sharing personal anecdotes and insights.

Promotion:

- Once your interviews are published, share them on your social media channels, website, and email newsletters.

---

5. Leveraging Book Reviews and Endorsements

Exercise: Book Review Campaign

Task: Reach out to book reviewers, bloggers, and influencers. Offer free copies of your book in exchange for honest reviews. Create a campaign to encourage readers to leave reviews on platforms like Amazon and Goodreads.

Goal: To gather positive reviews and endorsements that enhance your book's credibility and appeal.

Example Review Campaign:

Request Reviews:

- Contact 30 book reviewers and bloggers who specialize in your genre, offering free copies in exchange for honest reviews.

Highlight Endorsements:

- Feature endorsements from well-known authors or industry experts on your book cover, website, and marketing materials.

Create a Review Campaign:

- Encourage readers to leave reviews on Amazon, Goodreads, and Barnes & Noble by running a campaign with incentives such as a book giveaway or exclusive content.

---

6. Organizing Public Appearances and Events

Exercise: Plan a Book Signing Tour

Task: Organize a series of book signings at local bookstores, libraries, and literary festivals. Promote these events through your social media channels, email newsletters, and local media.

Goal: To connect with readers in person and promote your book through direct interaction.

Example Book Signing Tour Plan:

Step 1: Identify Venues

- List 10 local bookstores, libraries, and literary festivals for potential book signings.

Step 2: Schedule Events

- Contact each venue to arrange dates and times for your book signings.

Step 3: Promote Events

- Create promotional materials, including flyers and social media posts, to announce your book signings.

Step 4: Engage at Events

- During book signings, engage with attendees by sharing personal stories, answering questions, and signing books.

---

7. Networking with Industry Professionals

Exercise: Attend Industry Events

Task: Participate in book fairs, literary festivals, writing conferences, and networking events. Engage with other authors, publishers, agents, and media representatives.

Goal: To build relationships and open doors to new opportunities within the industry.

Example Industry Event Plan:

Step 1: Identify Events

- Research and list 5 upcoming industry events relevant to your genre.

Step 2: Register and Prepare

- Register for the events and prepare your materials, including business cards, press kits, and a brief introduction about yourself and your book.

Step 3: Engage and Network

- Attend the events, actively participate in discussions, and network with other attendees.

Step 4: Follow-Up

- After the events, follow up with new contacts to maintain and strengthen relationships.

---

8. Utilizing Social Media for PR

Exercise: Social Media PR Campaign

Task: Create a social media campaign to promote your media coverage, interviews, and public appearances. Use relevant hashtags, engage with followers, and run contests and giveaways.

Goal: To amplify your PR efforts and increase engagement with your audience.

Example Social Media PR Campaign:

Share Media Coverage:

- Post links to your media coverage, interviews, and reviews on all social media platforms. Tag the media outlets and journalists to increase visibility.

Engage with Followers:

- Respond to comments, participate in discussions, and share behind-the-scenes content related to your PR activities.

Use Hashtags:

- Utilize relevant hashtags to increase the discoverability of your posts. Create a unique hashtag for your book.

Run Contests and Giveaways:

- Host a contest or giveaway related to your book, encouraging participants to share your posts for additional entries.

By completing these exercises, you will effectively leverage media and public appearances to promote your book, build credibility, and connect with a broader audience. These PR strategies will help you enhance your book's visibility and establish your reputation as an author.

Exercises for Budgeting for Success: Creating a Budget for Your Book Publishing Journey

1. Estimate Your Costs

Exercise: Detailed Cost Estimation

Task: Break down the costs associated with each stage of your book publishing journey. Create a comprehensive list of potential expenses under the categories of writing-related expenses, production costs, marketing expenses, and distribution fees.

Goal: To gain a clear understanding of the financial requirements for publishing your book.

Example Breakdown:

Writing-Related Expenses:

- Research: $100 (books, subscriptions)
- Writing Tools: $50 (Scrivener, Grammarly)

Production Costs:

- Editing: $1,500 (developmental editing, copyediting, proofreading)
- Cover Design: $300
- Interior Formatting: $200
- Illustrations: $500
- ISBNs: $125 (one for print, one for digital)

Marketing Expenses:

- Book Launch: $200 (virtual event)
- Advertising: $300 (Facebook ads, Amazon ads)
- PR and Promotions: $400 (publicist fees, promotional campaigns)
- Review Copies: $100
- Marketing Materials: $150 (flyers, bookmarks)

Distribution Fees:

- Print-On-Demand: $100 (Amazon KDP, IngramSpark fees)
- Ebook Distribution: $50 (Amazon, Apple Books, Kobo fees)
- Shipping: $100

2. Set Financial Goals

Exercise: Financial Goal Setting

Task: Define your financial goals for your book publishing journey. Include revenue targets, break-even points, and profit margins. Create a plan to achieve these goals.

Goal: To stay focused on your financial objectives and measure your success.

Example Goals:

Revenue Targets:

- Aim to earn $5,000 from book sales in the first year.

Break-Even Point:

- Calculate the break-even point: Total Costs = $4,075 (sum of all expenses). Therefore, you need to sell enough books to cover this amount.

Profit Margin:

- Target a 20% profit margin after reaching the break-even point.

3. Allocate Funds Wisely

Exercise: Budget Allocation Plan

Task: Prioritize and allocate funds to different aspects of your book publishing journey based on their impact on success. Identify high, medium, and low priority areas.

Goal: To ensure that your budget is spent wisely, maximizing the impact on your book's success.

Example Allocation:

High Priority:

- Editing: $1,500
- Cover Design: $300

Medium Priority:

- Marketing: $1,000
- Formatting: $200

Low Priority:

- Additional Features: $150 (custom illustrations, high-end marketing materials)

---

4. Track Your Spending

Exercise: Expense Tracking Spreadsheet

Task: Create a spreadsheet to track all your book-related expenses. Record every expense, categorize them, and regularly review the totals.

Goal: To stay within your budget and make informed financial decisions throughout your publishing journey.

Example Spreadsheet:

Category	Item	Estimated Cost	Actual Cost	Notes
Writing-Related	Research	$100	$120	Extra database subscription
Production	Editing	$1,500	$1,450	
Marketing	Facebook Ads	$200	$250	Adjusted budget
Distribution	Print-On-Demand Fees	$100	$100	
Contingencies	Emergency Fund	$500	$450	Used for additional editing

5. Plan for Contingencies

Exercise: Emergency Fund Allocation

Task: Allocate a portion of your budget (10-15%) as an emergency fund for unforeseen expenses. Identify areas where you can reallocate funds if necessary.

Goal: To be prepared for unexpected costs and ensure the smooth progression of your publishing journey.

Example Plan:

Emergency Fund:

- Set aside $500 (12% of total budget).

Flexible Spending:

- Identify non-essential areas to reallocate funds if needed, such as reducing marketing materials from $150 to $100 if an emergency arises.

6. Analyze and Adjust

Exercise: Post-Publication Financial Analysis

Task: After publishing your book, analyze your actual expenses and revenue. Compare these against your initial budget and financial goals. Identify areas for improvement and adjust your budget for future projects.

Goal: To learn from your experience and improve your budgeting process for future projects.

Example Analysis:

Financial Analysis:

- Total Costs: $4,300 (compared to estimated $4,075)
- Total Revenue: $6,000 (compared to target $5,000)
- Profit: $1,700

Trends and Insights:

- Overspent on advertising but it yielded higher revenue.
- Underestimated the cost of research tools.

Adjust Future Budgets:

- Increase budget allocation for advertising based on its high return.
- Plan for higher research tool costs.

By completing these exercises, you will create a detailed and flexible budget that sets you up for success in your book publishing journey. This structured approach will help you manage your expenses, prioritize spending, and make informed financial decisions, ensuring your book's financial and commercial success.

Worksheets for Essential Investments: Identifying Key Areas Where Spending Money Can Enhance Your Book's Quality and Reach

1. Professional Editing

Exercise: Editing Cost Estimation Worksheet

Task: Estimate the costs for developmental editing, copyediting, and proofreading based on your manuscript length. Use industry-standard rates to calculate your budget for each editing stage.

Goal: To ensure your manuscript is polished and professional, enhancing readability and credibility.

Worksheet Example:

Manuscript Length: 80,000 words

Editing Type	Rate Per Word	Estimated Cost	Notes
Developmental Editing	$0.05	$4,000	Focus on structure, plot, and character development
Copyediting	$0.03	$2,400	Corrects grammar, punctuation, and syntax

Editing Type	Rate Per Word	Estimated Cost	Notes
Proofreading	$0.02	$1,600	Final check for typos and minor errors

2. Cover Design

Exercise: Cover Design Planning Worksheet

Task: Research and select a professional cover designer. Outline your design vision and estimate the cost based on the designer's rates.

Goal: To create a compelling cover that attracts readers and boosts sales.

Worksheet Example:

Designer: Jane Doe Designs

Design Element	Description	Estimated Cost	Notes
Front Cover	Custom illustration and typography	$500	Reflects the book's theme and genre
Back Cover	Blurb, author photo, and design	$200	Cohesive with front cover
Spine	Title and author name design	$100	Matches overall cover design

3. Interior Formatting

Exercise: Formatting Cost Estimation Worksheet

Task: Determine the costs for both print and ebook formatting services. Select a professional formatter and outline your requirements.

Goal: To ensure your book is professionally formatted for readability in both print and digital formats.

Worksheet Example:

Formatter: Formatting Pros

Formatting Type	Estimated Cost	Notes
Print Formatting	$300	Ensures proper margins, fonts, and spacing
Ebook Formatting	$200	Compatible with various e-readers and platforms

4. Illustrations and Graphics

Exercise: Illustration Planning Worksheet

Task: Plan and budget for any illustrations or graphics needed for your book. Select a professional illustrator and outline the required artwork.

Goal: To enhance your book's visual appeal and value with high-quality illustrations.

Worksheet Example:

Illustrator: Art by Anna

Illustration Type	Description	Estimated Cost	Notes
Cover Illustration	Full-color cover art	$400	Eye-catching and genre-appropriate
Interior Illustrations	10 black-and-white chapter headers	$1,000	Simple, complementing the text

5. ISBN and Distribution

Exercise: ISBN and Distribution Cost Worksheet

Task: Calculate the costs for obtaining ISBNs and setting up distribution through print-on-demand services.

Goal: To ensure your book is properly registered and widely available to readers.

Worksheet Example:

Item	Estimated Cost	Notes
ISBNs (10-pack)	$295	Covers multiple editions (print, ebook)
Amazon KDP Setup	Free	No upfront costs, per-copy printing fees apply
IngramSpark Setup	$49	Includes print setup, distribution to bookstores

6. Marketing and Promotion

Exercise: Marketing Budget Planning Worksheet

Task: Allocate your marketing budget to different promotional activities. Prioritize high-impact strategies and estimate costs for each.

Goal: To effectively promote your book and reach your target audience.

Worksheet Example:

Marketing Activity	Estimated Cost	Notes
Book Launch Event	$500	Includes venue, refreshments, and promotion
Social Media Advertising	$300/month	Targeted ads on Facebook and Instagram
Public Relations Campaign	$1,000	Hiring a publicist for media outreach

7. Author Website

Exercise: Website Development Worksheet

Task: Plan and budget for the creation of a professional author website. Include costs for design, domain registration, and hosting.

Goal: To establish a strong online presence and engage with your readers.

Worksheet Example:

Website Developer: WebWizards

Website Element	Estimated Cost	Notes
Design	$1,000	Custom design reflecting your brand
Domain Registration	$15/year	Secure a memorable domain name
Hosting	$85/year	Reliable hosting service

8. Book Reviews and Endorsements

Exercise: Review and Endorsement Campaign Worksheet

Task: Plan a campaign to send out review copies and secure endorsements. Budget for review copy costs and promotional materials.

Goal: To gather positive reviews and endorsements that enhance your book's credibility.

Worksheet Example:

Campaign Element	Estimated Cost	Notes
Review Copies	$200	Print and digital copies for reviewers
Endorsement Outreach	$100	Personalized packages for potential endorsers

9. Professional Associations and Memberships

Exercise: Association Membership Planning Worksheet

Task: Identify relevant professional associations and calculate the membership fees. Outline the benefits of joining each organization.

Goal: To access valuable resources, networking opportunities, and enhance your credibility.

Worksheet Example:

Association	Annual Fee	Benefits
Authors Guild	$125	Legal support, industry news, networking
Romance Writers of America	$99	Workshops, conferences, community support
Society of Children's Book Writers and Illustrators (SCBWI)	$80	Industry insights, marketing opportunities

By completing these worksheets, you will be able to allocate your budget effectively, ensuring that you invest in key areas that enhance your book's quality and reach. These structured plans will help you manage your finances wisely, leading to a successful and professional publication.

Worksheets for Cost-Effective Solutions: Finding Affordable Alternatives for Various Publishing Expenses

1. Freelance Services

Exercise: Freelance Services Planning Worksheet

Task: Identify and select freelancers for editing and cover design. Use platforms like Upwork, Fiverr, and 99designs to find professionals with competitive rates.

Goal: To access professional services at a lower cost than established firms.

Worksheet Example:

Editing Services:

Service	Freelancer/Platform	Rate Per Word	Estimated Cost (80,000 words)	Notes
Developmental Editing	Upwork	$0.02	$1,600	Highly rated editor in your genre
Copyediting	Fiverr	$0.015	$1,200	Experienced editor with good reviews
Proofreading	Reedsy	$0.01	$800	Specialized in final proofreading

Cover Design:

Designer/Platform	Cost	Notes
99designs	$300	Professional cover design contest

Designer/Platform	Cost	Notes
Fiverr	$150	Freelance designer with a strong portfolio
DeviantArt	$100	Talented artist offering custom designs

2. DIY Options

Exercise: DIY Formatting and Design Worksheet

Task: Plan to use DIY tools for formatting and cover design. Select software and outline steps to complete these tasks yourself.

Goal: To save money by doing some tasks yourself without compromising on quality.

Worksheet Example:

Formatting Tools:

Tool	Cost	Notes
Scrivener	$49	One-time purchase, versatile for both print and ebook formatting
Vellum	$199	User-friendly, professional-quality ebook formatting
Adobe InDesign	$20/month	Subscription, powerful design capabilities

Cover Design Tools:

Tool	Cost	Notes

Tool	Cost	Notes
Canva	Free/$12.95/month	Templates available for easy cover design
Adobe Photoshop	$20/month	Advanced design features for custom covers

3. Barter and Trade

Exercise: Barter and Trade Services Worksheet

Task: Identify skills you can trade with other authors or creatives. Outline potential barter agreements for services like editing, design, and marketing.

Goal: To reduce costs by exchanging services with other professionals.

Worksheet Example:

Service Needed	Service Offered	Potential Partner	Notes
Developmental Editing	Graphic Design Services	Fellow author, Jane Doe	Jane provides editing, you create her book cover
Beta Reading	Social Media Management	Writing group member	Exchange beta reading for managing their social media accounts
Marketing	Website Design	Freelance editor	Offer website design in exchange for a marketing strategy

4. Pre-made Covers

Exercise: Pre-made Cover Selection Worksheet

Task: Explore online marketplaces for pre-made book covers. Choose a cover that fits your book's theme and budget.

Goal: To obtain a professional-looking cover at a lower cost than custom designs.

Worksheet Example:

Marketplace	Cover Design	Cost	Notes
The Book Cover Designer	Fantasy Novel Cover #1	$75	Matches your book's genre and theme
SelfPubBookCovers	Romance Cover #3	$100	High-quality design, affordable price
GoOnWrite	Thriller Cover #2	$50	Visually appealing, cost-effective

5. Print-on-Demand Services

Exercise: Print-on-Demand Planning Worksheet

Task: Plan your use of print-on-demand (POD) services for both print and digital editions. Compare options and costs for Amazon KDP and IngramSpark.

Goal: To reduce upfront printing costs and manage financial risk.

Worksheet Example:

POD Service	Setup Fee	Per-Copy Cost	Notes
Amazon KDP	Free	Varies by book size	No upfront costs, wide distribution network
IngramSpark	$49	Varies by book size	Setup fee, wider bookstore distribution

6. Affordable Marketing and Promotion

Exercise: Marketing Budget Worksheet

Task: Plan affordable marketing strategies. Allocate budget for social media marketing, email marketing, and book review services.

Goal: To effectively promote your book without overspending.

Worksheet Example:

Marketing Strategy	Tool/Service	Cost	Notes
Social Media Marketing	Organic Posts	Free	Consistent posting and engagement
Paid Advertising	Facebook Ads	$100/month	Targeted ads to reach specific demographics
Email Marketing	Mailchimp	Free/$10/month	Build and maintain an email list
Book Review Services	BookSirens	$50	Affordable package for reviewer

Marketing Strategy	Tool/Service	Cost	Notes
			outreach

7. Libraries and Community Resources

Exercise: Community Promotion Planning Worksheet

Task: Identify local libraries and community centers for potential events. Plan author talks, book signings, and workshops.

Goal: To leverage local resources for cost-effective promotion.

Worksheet Example:

Venue	Event Type	Cost	Notes
Local Library	Author Talk	Free	Schedule a talk about your book and writing process
Community Center	Book Signing	Free	Partner with community centers for signings
Literary Festival	Workshop	Free/$50	Offer workshops at local literary festivals

8. Crowdfunding

Exercise: Crowdfunding Campaign Planning Worksheet

Task: Plan a crowdfunding campaign to cover publishing expenses. Outline rewards and set funding goals on platforms like Kickstarter or Indiegogo.

Goal: To raise funds and generate early interest in your book.

Worksheet Example:

Platform	Funding Goal	Campaign Duration	Notes
Kickstarter	$2,000	30 days	Offer rewards like signed copies, exclusive content
Indiegogo	$3,000	45 days	Flexible funding, offer tiered rewards

9. Grants and Contests

Exercise: Grant and Contest Application Worksheet

Task: Research and apply for writing grants and contests. List potential opportunities and application requirements.

Goal: To secure funding and recognition for your writing.

Worksheet Example:

Opportunity	Application Deadline	Prize/Funding	Notes
National Endowment for the Arts	March 1	$10,000	Research eligibility and application process

Opportunity	Application Deadline	Prize/Funding	Notes
Local Arts Council Grant	April 15	$1,500	Check local council for guidelines
Writing Contest	June 30	$500 + publication	Entry fee $25, focus on your book's genre

By completing these worksheets, you can find cost-effective solutions to manage your publishing expenses while maintaining high standards. These strategies will help you make informed decisions, ensuring a successful and budget-friendly publishing journey.

Exercises for Avoiding Common Financial Pitfalls in Publishing

1. Overestimating Sales

Exercise: Realistic Sales Projections Worksheet

Task: Research similar books in your genre to estimate realistic sales numbers. Create a sales projection for your book's first year.

Goal: To avoid overestimating sales and manage your inventory and marketing budget effectively.

Worksheet Example:

Book Title	Genre	Sales in First Year	Notes
Comparable Book 1	Fantasy	500 copies	Author's debut novel, moderate marketing
Comparable Book 2	Fantasy	1,200 copies	Strong social media presence
Comparable Book 3	Fantasy	800 copies	Featured in several blogs

Your Book's Projection:

Month	Projected Sales	Cumulative Sales	Notes
January	50	50	Initial launch
February	70	120	Post-launch promotions
March	80	200	Ongoing marketing efforts
April	90	290	Increased social media activity
...	...	...	...
December	100	900	Year-end push

2. Skipping Professional Services

Exercise: Service Provider Comparison Worksheet

Task: Obtain and compare quotes from several service providers for editing, cover design, and formatting.

Goal: To ensure you get quality services at a fair price.

Worksheet Example:

Editing Services:

Editor Name	Platform	Service Type	Rate Per Word	Estimated Cost (80,000 words)	Reviews/Rating
Editor A	Upwork	Developmental	$0.02	$1,600	4.8/5 from 100 reviews
Editor B	Reedsy	Copyediting	$0.015	$1,200	4.9/5 from 50 reviews
Editor C	Freelance	Proofreading	$0.01	$800	4.7/5 from 80 reviews

Cover Design:

Designer Name	Platform	Service Type	Cost	Portfolio Link	Reviews/Rating
Designer A	99designs	Custom Cover	$500	Portfolio	5/5 from 30 reviews
Designer B	Fiverr	Pre-made Cover	$150	Portfolio	4.8/5 from 50 reviews
Designer C	DeviantArt	Custom Artwork	$300	Portfolio	4.9/5 from 40 reviews

3. Ignoring Marketing

Exercise: Marketing Budget Allocation Worksheet

Task: Allocate a specific budget for various marketing activities. Include both free and paid strategies.

Goal: To ensure effective marketing without overspending.

Worksheet Example:

Marketing Activity	Cost	Notes
Social Media Ads	$200/month	Targeted Facebook and Instagram ads
Email Marketing (Mailchimp)	$20/month	Monthly newsletter to subscribers
Book Launch Event	$300	Venue, refreshments, and promotional materials
Free Marketing Channels	$0	Social media posts, blog articles, and interviews
Total Monthly Marketing Budget	$520	

---

4. Not Tracking Expenses

Exercise: Expense Tracking Worksheet

Task: Use a spreadsheet to track all book-related expenses. Regularly update and review your records.

Goal: To avoid overspending and ensure budget management.

Worksheet Example:

Date	Category	Description	Cost	Cumulative Total
Jan 5	Editing	Developmental Editing	$1,600	$1,600
Jan 15	Cover Design	Custom Cover	$500	$2,100
Feb 1	Marketing	Facebook Ads	$200	$2,300
Feb 10	Formatting	Print Formatting	$300	$2,600
...	...	...	...	...

5. Underpricing Your Book

Exercise: Pricing Strategy Worksheet

Task: Research the pricing of comparable books in your genre and test different price points.

Goal: To set a competitive price that covers costs and provides a profit margin.

Worksheet Example:

Comparable Book Title	Genre	Price	Notes
Book 1	Fantasy	$12.99	Similar length and quality
Book 2	Fantasy	$14.99	Well-known author
Book 3	Fantasy	$9.99	Indie author, lower price

Comparable Book Title	Genre	Price point	Notes

Your Book Pricing Strategy:

Price Point	Duration	Sales Volume	Revenue	Notes
$9.99	1 month	100 copies	$999	Initial launch, attract new readers
$12.99	2 months	150 copies	$1,949	Regular price, competitive
$14.99	1 month	75 copies	$1,124	Test higher price point

6. Overcommitting Financially

Exercise: Realistic Budget Planning Worksheet

Task: Create a detailed budget based on your financial capacity and set a contingency fund for unexpected expenses.

Goal: To avoid financial strain and ensure sustainable publishing efforts.

Worksheet Example:

Expense Category	Budget Limit	Actual Spending	Notes
Editing	$2,000	$1,800	Stayed within budget
Cover Design	$600	$500	Under budget
Marketing	$1,200	$1,300	Slightly over budget

Expense Category	Budget Limit	Actual Spending	Notes
Contingency Fund	$500	$450	Used for additional editing
Total	$4,300	$4,050	Stayed within overall budget

7. Not Planning for Long-Term Financial Health

Exercise: Long-Term Financial Planning Worksheet

Task: Plan for multiple revenue streams and allocate a portion of your earnings for future projects and personal savings.

Goal: To ensure long-term financial stability and growth.

Worksheet Example:

Revenue Stream	Projected Earnings	Notes
Book Sales	$5,000	Based on conservative sales projections
Audiobook Sales	$2,000	Additional format to reach more readers
Foreign Rights	$1,500	Potential earnings from foreign publishers
Merchandise	$500	Branded merchandise related to your book
Total Projected Revenue	$9,000	

Savings and Investments:

Allocation	Amount	Notes
Future Projects	$3,000	Set aside for next book
Personal Savings	$2,000	Emergency fund and savings
Marketing Reserve	$1,000	For ongoing promotional activities
Education/Training	$500	Courses and workshops
Total Savings	$6,500	

8. Failing to Seek Professional Financial Advice

Exercise: Financial Advisory Planning Worksheet

Task: Identify the need for financial advice and plan consultations with a financial advisor or accountant.

Goal: To manage your finances effectively and ensure compliance with financial regulations.

Worksheet Example:

Advisor/Service	Cost	Notes
Financial Advisor	$150/hour	Consultation on budgeting and investing
Accountant	$500/year	Annual tax filing and financial management
Total	$650	

9. Overlooking the Cost of Time

Exercise: Time Management Worksheet

Task: Track the time spent on various publishing tasks and evaluate whether outsourcing certain tasks would be beneficial.

Goal: To optimize your workflow and focus on high-priority activities.

Worksheet Example:

Task	Time Spent (hours)	Outsource?	Notes
Writing	20	No	Core activity, high priority
Social Media Management	10	Yes	Time-consuming, can be outsourced
Formatting	8	No	DIY to save costs
Marketing Strategy	15	Yes	Hire a professional marketer
Total Weekly Hours	53		

By completing these exercises, you will be better prepared to navigate the financial aspects of publishing and avoid common pitfalls. These strategies will help you manage your budget effectively, ensuring a smooth and successful publishing journey.

Query Letter Example

[Your Name]
[Your Address]
[City, State, ZIP Code]
[Email Address]
[Phone Number]
[Date]

[Agent's Name]
[Agency's Name]
[Agency's Address]
[City, State, ZIP Code]

Dear [Agent's Name],

Hook: When renowned detective Jane Doe discovers a cryptic message in a murder victim's diary, she embarks on a dangerous quest to unravel a conspiracy that could shake the city's foundations.

Book Summary: In *Whispers in the Wind*, young archaeologist Emma Collins discovers an ancient artifact that holds the key to a forgotten civilization. As she delves deeper into its mysteries, she must navigate treacherous terrain, rival treasure hunters, and a looming threat that endangers everything she holds dear. With the help of enigmatic historian Jack Reynolds, Emma uncovers secrets that could rewrite history—but only if they can survive long enough to reveal the truth.

Author Bio: I am a graduate of the Iowa Writers' Workshop, where I honed my skills in literary fiction. My short stories have been published in *The New Yorker* and *The Atlantic*, and I am a recipient of the Pushcart Prize. Currently, I teach creative writing at the University of Washington. *Whispers in the Wind* is inspired by my own adventures in archaeology and my passion for uncovering hidden histories.

Closing: Thank you for considering *Whispers in the Wind*. I am happy to provide the full manuscript, a detailed synopsis, or any additional information upon request. I look forward to the possibility of working with you.

Sincerely,
[Your Name]

Exercise: Fix the Query Letter

Instructions: Below is a query letter that contains several issues. Review the letter and rewrite it to improve the hook, book summary, author bio, and closing.

[Your Name]
[Your Address]
[City, State, ZIP Code]
[Email Address]

[Phone Number]
[Date]

[Agent's Name]
[Agency's Name]
[Agency's Address]
[City, State, ZIP Code]

Dear [Agent's Name],

Hook: My book is about a young archaeologist named Emma who finds an artifact.

Book Summary: In my book, *Whispers in the Wind*, Emma Collins finds an artifact. She has to deal with some challenges and threats while trying to understand it. She meets Jack, a historian, and they work together. They find out some important stuff that could change history.

Author Bio: I like archaeology and have written a few short stories. This is my first novel.

Closing: I hope you like my book. Let me know if you want to see more.

Thanks,
[Your Name]

Revised Query Letter:

[Your Name]
[Your Address]
[City, State, ZIP Code]
[Email Address]
[Phone Number]
[Date]

[Agent's Name]
[Agency's Name]
[Agency's Address]
[City, State, ZIP Code]

Dear [Agent's Name],

Hook: When young archaeologist Emma Collins unearths an ancient artifact, she unknowingly triggers a series of events that could alter the course of history.

Book Summary: In *Whispers in the Wind*, Emma Collins' discovery of a mysterious artifact sends her on a thrilling journey fraught with danger and intrigue. Navigating through perilous terrains and dodging ruthless treasure hunters, Emma partners with enigmatic historian Jack Reynolds. Together, they unveil secrets that have the power to rewrite the history of a long-lost civilization. Their mission, however, becomes a race against time as they face escalating threats that put their lives and their newfound knowledge at risk.

Author Bio: With a passion for archaeology, I have channeled my real-life adventures into my writing. A graduate of the Iowa Writers' Workshop, my short stories have been featured in *The New Yorker* and *The Atlantic*. I am also a Pushcart Prize recipient and currently teach creative writing at the University of Washington. *Whispers in the Wind* is my debut novel, inspired by my love for uncovering hidden histories.

Closing: Thank you for considering *Whispers in the Wind*. I am excited to share the full manuscript, a detailed synopsis, or any additional information you may need. I look forward to the opportunity of working with you.

Sincerely,
[Your Name]

Additional Exercises for Query Letter Writing

Analyze Successful Query Letters:

1. **Task:** Find and analyze three successful query letters in your genre. Identify the elements that make them compelling and note the structure, tone, and key phrases used.
2. **Goal:** To understand what works in successful query letters and apply similar techniques to your own.

Write Multiple Hooks:

1. **Task:** Write five different hooks for your manuscript. Choose the one that is most captivating and reflective of your book's tone and style.
2. **Goal:** To refine your hook and ensure it effectively grabs the reader's attention.

Peer Review:

1. **Task:** Exchange query letters with a peer or writing group member. Provide constructive feedback on each other's letters.
2. **Goal:** To gain an outside perspective and improve the clarity and impact of your query letter.

Revise and Refine:

1. **Task:** Write a draft of your query letter and revise it at least three times, focusing on different elements (hook, book summary, author bio, closing) in each revision.
2. **Goal:** To produce a polished and compelling query letter through iterative improvements.

By practicing these exercises, you will enhance your query letter writing skills and increase your chances of catching the interest of literary agents and publishers.

Outstanding Query Letter Template

[Your Name]
[Your Address]
[City, State, ZIP Code]
[Email Address]
[Phone Number]
[Date]

[Agent's Name]
[Agency's Name]
[Agency's Address]
[City, State, ZIP Code]

Dear [Agent's Name],

Hook: [Insert a compelling, attention-grabbing opening that encapsulates the essence of your book. Example: "When [Protagonist's Name], a [Brief Description of Protagonist], uncovers [Key Event or Discovery], they must [Action/Decision/Conflict] or face [Consequences]."]

Book Summary:

Paragraph 1: [Briefly introduce the main character(s) and the setting. Example: "In [Book Title], [Protagonist's Name] is a [Occupation/Role] in [Setting/Time Period]. Their life takes an unexpected turn when they discover [Inciting Incident]."]

Paragraph 2: [Describe the main conflict or challenge, including the antagonist if applicable. Example: "As [Protagonist's Name] delves deeper into [Discovery/Event], they must confront [Antagonist/Conflict], navigating through [Challenges/Obstacles]."]

Paragraph 3: [Highlight the stakes and what the protagonist stands to gain or lose. Example: "With [High Stakes] at risk, [Protagonist's Name] must [Climactic Decision/Action] to [Goal/Resolution]. Will they succeed before [Critical Deadline/Consequence]?"]

Author Bio:

[Insert your writing background, relevant experience, and notable achievements. Example: "I am a graduate of [Writing Program/Workshop], where I honed my skills in [Genre]. My work has been published in [Notable Publications], and I have received [Awards/Recognition]. [Book Title] is inspired by [Personal Connection/Expertise Related to the Book's Theme]."]

Closing:

[Thank the agent and invite them to request additional materials. Example: "Thank you for considering [Book Title]. I am happy to provide the full manuscript, a detailed synopsis, or any additional information upon request. I look forward to the possibility of working with you."]

Sincerely,
[Your Name]

Fill-in-the-Blank Example

[Your Name]
[123 Writer's Lane]
[Booktown, BK 12345]
[youremail@example.com]
[555-123-4567]
[June 19, 2024]

Ms. Jane Agent
Literary Talent Agency
456 Publishing Ave.
Literary City, LC 67890

Dear Ms. Agent,

Hook: When aspiring journalist Emma Blake uncovers a hidden diary from World War II, she must unravel its secrets before a shadowy organization erases the past forever.

Book Summary:

Paragraph 1: In *Echoes of Silence*, Emma Blake is a determined journalist in modern-day London. Her life takes an unexpected turn when she discovers an old diary hidden in the walls of her late grandmother's attic.

Paragraph 2: As Emma delves deeper into the diary's contents, she uncovers a story of espionage and betrayal during World War II. She must confront a powerful organization determined to keep these secrets buried, while navigating the moral complexities of exposing the past.

Paragraph 3: With her career and the truth on the line, Emma must race against time to reveal the diary's secrets. If she fails, a significant part of history may be lost forever, and those responsible for the wartime treachery may never be held accountable.

Author Bio:

I am a graduate of the University of Oxford's Creative Writing program, where I specialized in historical fiction. My work has been published in *The Historical Journal* and *Literary Review*, and I have received the Historical Fiction Award from the Writers' Guild. *Echoes of Silence* is inspired by my passion for uncovering untold stories from the past and my background in journalism.

Closing:

Thank you for considering *Echoes of Silence*. I am happy to provide the full manuscript, a detailed synopsis, or any additional information upon request. I look forward to the possibility of working with you.

Sincerely,
Emma Writer

This template is designed to be adaptable for any book and author, allowing you to tailor each section to fit your manuscript's unique elements and your personal achievements. By filling in the blanks with your specific details, you can create a query letter that stands out and grabs the attention of literary agents and publishers.

Exercises for Writing an Effective Query Letter

Exercise 1: Keeping It Concise and Focused

Task: Write a query letter for your manuscript, ensuring it does not exceed one page. Focus only on the hook, book summary, author bio, and closing.

Goal: To practice brevity and relevance in your query letter.

Example Worksheet:

Section	Word Count	Content
Hook	1-2 sentences	"When [Protagonist] discovers [Key Event], they must [Action/Decision/Conflict] or face [Consequences]."

Section	Word Count	Content
Book Summary	150-200 words	"In [Book Title], [Protagonist's Name] is a [Occupation/Role] in [Setting/Time Period]. Their life takes an unexpected turn when [Inciting Incident]. As they delve deeper into [Discovery/Event], they must confront [Antagonist/Conflict], navigating through [Challenges/Obstacles]. With [High Stakes] at risk, [Protagonist's Name] must [Climactic Decision/Action] to [Goal/Resolution]. Will they succeed before [Critical Deadline/Consequence]?"
Author Bio	1-2 paragraphs	"I am a graduate of [Writing Program/Workshop], where I honed my skills in [Genre]. My work has been published in [Notable Publications], and I have received [Awards/Recognition]. [Book Title] is inspired by [Personal Connection/Expertise Related to the Book's Theme]."
Closing	1-2 sentences	"Thank you for considering [Book Title]. I am happy to provide the full manuscript, a detailed synopsis, or any additional information upon request. I look forward to the possibility of working with you."

Exercise 2: Following Submission Guidelines

Task: Research submission guidelines for three different agents or publishers and write a query letter tailored to one of them. Ensure you follow their specific guidelines precisely.

Goal: To understand the importance of adhering to submission requirements and customize your query letter accordingly.

Example Worksheet:

Agent/Publisher	Guidelines Summary	Compliance Notes
Agent A	Accepts email queries only, include first 10 pages in the body of the email. Max 300 words.	"Query sent via email. Added first 10 pages below the query letter. Kept the query letter to 300 words."
Agent B	Requires a query letter, synopsis, and first 3 chapters as attachments.	"Attached query letter, synopsis, and first 3 chapters as separate documents. Followed their preferred formatting for attachments."
Publisher C	Online form submission only, no email queries. Specific questions to answer in the submission form.	"Submitted query via online form. Answered all required questions and uploaded the query letter in the designated field. Followed character limits."

Exercise 3: Personalizing Your Query

Task: Write a personalized query letter for an agent or publisher, including specific reasons why you chose to query them. Highlight any connections between your manuscript and their interests.

Goal: To demonstrate the importance of personalization in a query letter.

Example Worksheet:

Section	Personalization Details
Salutation	"Dear [Agent's Name],"
Personalization	"I am querying you because of your interest in [specific genre or theme]. Your work with [Author or Book Title] inspired me to reach out, as my book shares similar themes of [relevant themes]."
Hook	"When [Protagonist] discovers [Key Event], they must [Action/Decision/Conflict] or face [Consequences]."
Book Summary	"In [Book Title], [Protagonist's Name] is a [Occupation/Role] in [Setting/Time Period]. Their life takes an unexpected turn when [Inciting Incident]. As they delve deeper into [Discovery/Event], they must confront [Antagonist/Conflict], navigating through [Challenges/Obstacles]. With [High Stakes] at risk, [Protagonist's Name] must [Climactic Decision/Action] to [Goal/Resolution]. Will they succeed before [Critical Deadline/Consequence]?"
Author Bio	"I am a graduate of [Writing

Section	Personalization Details
	Program/Workshop], where I honed my skills in [Genre]. My work has been published in [Notable Publications], and I have received [Awards/Recognition]. [Book Title] is inspired by [Personal Connection/Expertise Related to the Book's Theme]."
Closing	"Thank you for considering [Book Title]. I am happy to provide the full manuscript, a detailed synopsis, or any additional information upon request. I look forward to the possibility of working with you."

Exercise 4: Proofreading and Editing

Task: Write a draft of your query letter and exchange it with a peer or mentor for feedback. Incorporate their suggestions and revise your letter.

Goal: To ensure your query letter is polished, free of errors, and professionally presented.

Example Worksheet:

Section	Feedback Received	Revisions Made
Hook	"The hook needs to be more compelling."	Revised hook to: "When [Protagonist] discovers [Key Event], they must [Action/Decision/Conflict] or face [Consequences]."
Book Summary	"Too vague, needs more	Added specific details: "As [Protagonist] delves deeper into

Section	Feedback Received	Revisions Made
	specifics about the conflict."	[Discovery/Event], they must confront [Antagonist/Conflict], navigating through [Challenges/Obstacles]."
Author Bio	"Expand on your relevant experience."	Included more details about writing credentials and relevant expertise.
Closing	"Good closing, but could be more engaging."	Enhanced closing to: "Thank you for considering [Book Title]. I am excited to share the full manuscript or any additional information you may need. I look forward to the possibility of working with you."

Exercise 5: Avoiding Common Mistakes

Task: Identify common mistakes in the following query letter and rewrite it to improve its effectiveness.

Mistake Letter:

css
Copy code
Hey Agent,

My book is about a cool archaeologist named Emma who finds a magical artifact. It's really interesting and I think you'll love it. I'm a writer with a few stories published here and there. Hope to hear from you soon!

Thanks, [Your Name]

Revised Letter Worksheet:

Section	Original Text	Revised Text
Salutation	"Hey Agent,"	"Dear [Agent's Name],"
Hook	"My book is about a cool archaeologist named Emma who finds a magical artifact."	"When archaeologist Emma Blake uncovers a hidden artifact, she must unravel its secrets before a shadowy organization erases history forever."
Book Summary	"It's really interesting and I think you'll love it."	"In *Whispers in the Wind*, Emma Blake's discovery of a mysterious artifact sends her on a thrilling journey fraught with danger and intrigue. As she delves deeper into the artifact's secrets, she must confront powerful enemies determined to keep the past buried, all while navigating the moral complexities of exposing long-hidden truths."
Author Bio	"I'm a writer with a few stories published here and there."	"I am a graduate of the University of Oxford's Creative Writing program, with short stories published in *The Historical Journal* and *Literary Review*. I have received the Historical Fiction Award from

Section	Original Text	Revised Text
		the Writers' Guild. *Whispers in the Wind* is inspired by my passion for archaeology and uncovering untold stories."
Closing	"Hope to hear from you soon! Thanks, [Your Name]"	"Thank you for considering *Whispers in the Wind*. I am happy to provide the full manuscript, a detailed synopsis, or any additional information upon request. I look forward to the possibility of working with you. Sincerely, [Your Name]"

By practicing these exercises, you will refine your ability to write effective query letters, enhance your professionalism, and improve your chances of capturing the interest of literary agents and publishers.

Exercises for Personalizing Your Query Letter

Exercise 1: Research Each Agent or Publisher

Task: Select three literary agents or publishers you are interested in querying. Conduct thorough research on each one to gather information about their preferences, represented authors, and submission guidelines.

Goal: To gather detailed information that will help you personalize your query letters effectively.

Example Worksheet:

Agent/Publisher	Preferences/Genres	Represented Authors	Submission Guidelines	Notes
Agent A	Contemporary Romance, Women's Fiction	Author X, Author Y	Email query, first 10 pages attached	Interested in strong, independent female protagonists and small-town settings
Publisher B	Historical Fiction, Mystery	Author Z	Online form, synopsis, first 3 chapters	Prefers manuscripts with well-researched historical backgrounds
Agent C	Sci-Fi, Fantasy	Author W	Email query, detailed synopsis, no attachments	Likes character-driven sci-fi with ethical dilemmas, enjoys epic fantasy with rich

Agent/Publisher	Preferences/Genres	Represented Authors	Submission Guidelines	Notes
				lore

Exercise 2: Personalize the Salutation

Task: Write personalized salutations for the agents or publishers you researched in Exercise 1.

Goal: To practice addressing your query letters specifically and respectfully.

Example Worksheet:

Agent/Publisher	Generic Salutation	Personalized Salutation
Agent A	"Dear Agent,"	"Dear Ms. [Agent's Last Name],"
Publisher B	"To Whom It May Concern,"	"Dear [Publisher's Last Name],"
Agent C	"Dear Sir/Madam,"	"Dear Mr. [Agent's Last Name],"

Exercise 3: Mention Why You're Querying Them

Task: Write the opening paragraph for your query letter to each agent or publisher, explaining why you chose to query them specifically.

Goal: To show that you have done your research and understand their preferences.

Example Worksheet:

Agent/Publisher	Opening Paragraph
Agent A	"Dear Ms. [Agent's Last Name], I am writing to you because of your interest in contemporary romance with strong, independent female protagonists. Given your successful representation of [Author Name] and your enthusiasm for stories set in small-town settings, I believe my novel 'Love in the Lakeside' would be a great addition to your list."
Publisher B	"Dear [Publisher's Last Name], I am excited to submit my historical fiction manuscript, 'Echoes of the Past,' for your consideration. Your work with [Author Name] and your preference for well-researched historical backgrounds resonate with the themes and depth of my novel."
Agent C	"Dear Mr. [Agent's Last Name], I am thrilled to query you with my character-driven sci-fi novel, 'Galactic Echoes.' Your interest in ethical dilemmas within sci-fi narratives, as seen in your representation of [Author Name], aligns perfectly with the central themes of my manuscript."

Exercise 4: Highlight Relevant Experience

Task: Tailor your author bio to each agent or publisher, emphasizing relevant experience or credentials.

Goal: To align your background with their interests and demonstrate your suitability as an author.

Example Worksheet:

Agent/Publisher	Generic Author Bio	Tailored Author Bio
Agent A	"I am an experienced writer with a passion for romance novels."	"As a member of the Romance Writers of America and a finalist in the Golden Heart Awards, my passion for contemporary romance with strong, independent female protagonists aligns with your interests. My previous novel, 'Love Blossoms,' was praised for its vivid small-town setting."
Publisher B	"I have a background in writing historical fiction."	"As a member of the Historical Novel Society and a contributor to 'Historical Fiction Review,' I have a deep passion for bringing the past to life. My previous novel, 'Echoes of the Past,' was nominated for the Historical Novel Award, reflecting my dedication to well-researched historical

Agent/Publisher	Generic Author Bio	Tailored Author Bio
Agent C	"I write science fiction and fantasy novels."	narratives." "With a degree in Astrophysics and experience as a contributor to 'Sci-Fi Monthly,' I bring a unique perspective to character-driven sci-fi. My previous work, 'Galactic Echoes,' explores ethical dilemmas in space exploration, aligning with your interest in rich, thought-provoking narratives."

Exercise 5: Tailor the Book Summary

Task: Adjust the book summary to emphasize elements that align with each agent's or publisher's interests.

Goal: To highlight aspects of your manuscript that resonate with their preferences.

Example Worksheet:

Agent/Publisher	Generic Book Summary	Tailored Book Summary
Agent A	"'Love in the Lakeside' is a contemporary	"'Love in the Lakeside' is a contemporary romance set in a charming small

Agent/Publisher	Generic Book Summary	Tailored Book Summary
	romance about Emma, who returns to her hometown to save her family's inn and finds love."	town, focusing on the journey of Emma, a fiercely independent woman who returns to her hometown to save her family's inn. The novel explores themes of community, resilience, and the rediscovery of love, which align with your interest in heartwarming, character-driven stories."
Publisher B	"'Echoes of the Past' is a historical fiction novel about an archaeologist uncovering secrets from World War II."	"'Echoes of the Past' is a meticulously researched historical fiction novel that follows archaeologist Emma Collins as she uncovers secrets from World War II. The novel delves into the complexities of history, memory, and the moral dilemmas faced by those uncovering the past, aligning with your preference for well-researched and thought-

Agent/Publisher	Generic Book Summary	Tailored Book Summary
Agent C	" 'Galactic Echoes' is a sci-fi novel about a space explorer facing ethical dilemmas on an uncharted planet."	provoking historical narratives." " 'Galactic Echoes' is a character-driven sci-fi novel that explores the ethical dilemmas faced by Captain Alex Turner as he navigates uncharted space. The story delves into themes of morality, choice, and the human condition, resonating with your interest in rich, thought-provoking narratives within the sci-fi genre."

Exercise 6: Follow Their Submission Guidelines

Task: Write a query letter for each agent or publisher, ensuring you adhere to their specific submission guidelines.

Goal: To demonstrate professionalism and respect for their submission process.

Example Worksheet:

Agent/Publisher	Submission Guidelines Summary	Query Letter Checklist

Agent/Publisher	Submission Guidelines Summary	Query Letter Checklist
Agent A	"Email query, include first 10 pages in the body of the email, max 300 words."	[ ] Email query [ ] First 10 pages in body of email [ ] Query letter under 300 words
Publisher B	"Online form submission, include synopsis and first 3 chapters."	[ ] Online form [ ] Synopsis included [ ] First 3 chapters attached
Agent C	"Email query, detailed synopsis, no attachments, max 500 words."	[ ] Email query [ ] Detailed synopsis in body of email [ ] No attachments [ ] Query letter under 500 words

Exercise 7: Express Genuine Interest

Task: Write a closing paragraph for your query letter, expressing your enthusiasm for the agent or publisher and the potential collaboration.

Goal: To convey your genuine interest and leave a positive impression.

Example Worksheet:

Agent/Publisher	Generic Closing	Personalized Closing
Agent A	"I hope to hear from you soon.	"I admire your dedication to nurturing new voices in contemporary romance, and I am

Agent/Publisher	Generic Closing	Personalized Closing
	Thank you."	excited about the possibility of collaborating with you to bring 'Love in the Lakeside' to readers who appreciate heartfelt, character-driven stories. Thank you for considering my manuscript."
Publisher B	"Looking forward to your response. Thanks."	"I am inspired by your commitment to publishing well-researched historical fiction and believe that 'Echoes of the Past' would be a valuable addition to your catalog. I look forward to the possibility of working together. Thank you for your time and consideration."
Agent C	"Thank you for your time. Hope to hear from you."	"Your passion for thought-provoking sci-fi narratives is truly inspiring, and I am excited about the potential to work together on 'Galactic Echoes.' Thank you for considering my manuscript. I look forward to your response."

By completing these exercises, you will enhance your ability to personalize query letters, making them more appealing to literary agents and publishers. Personalization demonstrates your professionalism, attention to detail, and genuine interest in building a working relationship, increasing your chances of a positive response.

Exercises for Analyzing Successful Query Letters

Exercise 1: Identify Key Components

Task: Review each of the three successful query letter examples provided. Identify and label the key components: the hook, the book summary, the author bio, and the closing.

Goal: To understand the structure and elements that make a query letter effective.

Example Worksheet:

Query Letter	Hook	Book Summary	Author Bio	Closing
Example 1: Contemporary Romance	When Emma Collins returns to her hometown of Lakeside to save her family's inn, she expects to face financial struggles—not to rediscover	In 'Love in the Lakeside,' Emma Collins, a fiercely independent woman, returns to the small town of Lakeside to prevent her family's	I am a graduate of the Iowa Writers' Workshop, where I honed my skills in crafting contemporary romance. My short stories have been published	Thank you for considering 'Love in the Lakeside.' I am happy to provide the full manuscript, a detailed synopsis, or any

Query Letter	Hook	Book Summary	Author Bio	Closing
	the love she left behind.	inn from closing. Facing financial difficulties and community opposition, Emma reluctantly teams up with Jack Harper, her high school sweetheart and the town's most eligible bachelor. As they work together to save the inn, old sparks reignite, and Emma	in 'The New Yorker' and 'The Atlantic,' and I am a recipient of the Pushcart Prize. Currently, I teach creative writing at the University of Washington. 'Love in the Lakeside' is inspired by my own experiences growing up in a small town and my passion for stories	additional information upon request. I look forward to the possibility of working with you.

Query Letter	Hook	Book Summary	Author Bio	Closing
		must decide whether to embrace the love she once ran from or continue her life of independence. The novel explores themes of community, resilience, and the rediscovery of love, which align with your interest in heartwarming, character-	that celebrate love and community.	

Query Letter	Hook	Book Summary	Author Bio	Closing
Example 2: Mystery/Thriller	When Detective Sarah Blake uncovers a series of cryptic messages in a murder victim's diary, she is thrust into a deadly game of cat and mouse with a cunning serial killer.	driven stories. 'Shadows of Deceit' follows Detective Sarah Blake as she investigates a string of brutal murders that have left the city of Seattle in fear. Each victim's diary contains a cryptic message that leads Sarah deeper into a web	I have a background in criminal psychology and have worked closely with law enforcement agencies on criminal profiling. My short fiction has appeared in 'Ellery Queen's Mystery Magazine,' and I am a member of the Mystery Writers of America. 'Shadows of Deceit' draws on my	Thank you for considering 'Shadows of Deceit.' I am excited to provide the full manuscript, a detailed synopsis, or any additional information upon your request. I look forward to the possibility of collaborat

Query Letter	Hook	Book Summary	Author Bio	Closing
		of deceit and danger. As she races against time to decode the messages, she discovers a chilling connection to her own past. With the help of forensic expert Dr. Jake Williams, Sarah must confront her deepest fears and outsmart a killer who is always one step	professional experience and passion for creating suspenseful, character-driven stories.	ing with you.

Query Letter	Hook	Book Summary	Author Bio	Closing
Example 3: Science Fiction	In a future where memories can be erased and rewritten, one woman must uncover the truth about her past to save humanity's future.	ahead. This novel combines high-stakes action with psychological depth, making it a perfect fit for your list. 'Eclipse of the Mind' is set in a dystopian future where the government controls the population by manipulating memories. Elena	I hold a degree in cognitive science and have published articles on memory and consciousness in scientific journals. My short stories have appeared in	Thank you for considering 'Eclipse of the Mind.' I am eager to provide the full manuscript, a detailed synopsis, or any additional

Query Letter	Hook	Book Summary	Author Bio	Closing
		Morgan, a former memory technician, discovers that her own memories have been tampered with, hiding a secret that could topple the regime. As she delves into the forbidden world of memory hacking, she joins forces with a group of rebels determined	'Asimov's Science Fiction' and 'Clarkesworld Magazine.' 'Eclipse of the Mind' combines my academic background with my love for speculative fiction, creating a thought-provoking and action-packed narrative.	information upon request. I look forward to the opportunity to work with you.

Query Letter	Hook	Book Summary	Author Bio	Closing
		to restore freedom. Together, they must navigate a treacherous landscape of deceit, betrayal, and hidden truths. The novel explores themes of identity, freedom, and the ethical implications of memory manipulation.		

Exercise 2: Breakdown and Analysis

Task: Write a detailed breakdown of why each key component in the query letters is effective. Discuss the strengths and impact of the hook, book summary, author bio, and closing.

Goal: To critically analyze the effectiveness of each component in capturing an agent's or publisher's attention.

Example Worksheet:

Query Letter	Component	Analysis
Example 1: Contemporary Romance	Hook	The hook is engaging and immediately sets up the central conflict and romance, making the reader curious about Emma's journey and the rekindled romance with Jack.
	Book Summary	The summary provides a clear overview of the plot, introducing the main characters and conflict while highlighting themes of community and love that align with the agent's interests.
	Author Bio	The bio showcases the author's credentials, including prestigious publications and awards, and connects their personal experiences to the book's themes, enhancing credibility.
	Closing	The closing is polite and professional, expressing

Query Letter	Component	Analysis
		gratitude and inviting further communication, which leaves a positive impression.
Example 2: Mystery/Thriller	Hook	The hook is intriguing and sets up a high-stakes conflict, immediately grabbing attention with the promise of a gripping thriller.
	Book Summary	The summary effectively outlines the plot and central conflict, highlighting the psychological depth and action, which are appealing to the agent.
	Author Bio	The bio emphasizes the author's relevant background in criminal psychology and previous publications, establishing expertise and credibility in the genre.
	Closing	The closing is professional and invites the agent to request more material, maintaining a courteous and enthusiastic tone.
Example 3: Science Fiction	Hook	The hook is compelling, presenting a high-concept premise that piques interest in the dystopian world and the protagonist's quest.
	Book	The summary provides a clear and

Query Letter	Component	Analysis
	Summary	engaging overview of the plot, characters, and themes, highlighting the novel's speculative elements and ethical questions.
	Author Bio	The bio emphasizes the author's relevant academic background and previous publications in the genre, enhancing credibility and showcasing expertise.
	Closing	The closing is polite and professional, inviting the agent to request more material and expressing eagerness to collaborate.

Exercise 3: Rewrite a Query Letter

Task: Take a poorly written query letter (provided below) and rewrite it to incorporate the successful elements identified in the examples.

Goal: To practice applying the principles of a strong query letter to improve a less effective one.

Poorly Written Query Letter:

css
Copy code
Dear Agent,

I wrote a mystery novel called 'Murder in the Dark.' It's about a detective who solves a murder. I think you might like it because it's a good story. I've never been published before, but I love writing.

Thanks, [Your Name]

Rewrite Worksheet:

Component	Poor Version	Improved Version
Hook	I wrote a mystery novel called 'Murder in the Dark.'	When Detective John Harris stumbles upon a chilling murder scene in the heart of the city, he uncovers a trail of deceit that threatens to unravel his own dark past.
Book Summary	It's about a detective who solves a murder.	'Murder in the Dark' follows Detective John Harris as he investigates a series of gruesome murders that have left the city in fear. Each clue leads him deeper into a web of deceit and corruption that reaches into the highest levels of power. As he gets closer to the truth, Harris discovers a personal connection to the case that forces him to confront his own haunted past. This mystery combines intense action with psychological depth, making it a perfect fit for your list.
Author	I've never	Although 'Murder in the Dark' is

Component	Poor Version	Improved Version
Bio	been published before, but I love writing.	my debut novel, I have honed my writing skills through extensive coursework in creative writing and criminology. I am a member of the Mystery Writers of America and have received mentorship from established authors in the genre. My background in criminology has provided me with a unique perspective on the psychological and procedural aspects of crime, which I have woven into this novel.
Closing	Thanks,	Thank you for considering 'Murder in the Dark.' I am excited to provide the full manuscript, a detailed synopsis, or any additional information upon your request. I look forward to the opportunity to work with you. Best regards, [Your Name]

Exercise 4: Write Your Own Query Letter

Task: Write a query letter for your own manuscript, applying the principles and structure learned from the examples and breakdowns.

Goal: To create a polished and effective query letter for your own manuscript.

Example Worksheet:

Component	Details
Hook	[Write your engaging hook here.]
Book Summary	[Summarize your book, highlighting key plot points, characters, and themes.]
Author Bio	[Provide relevant background, writing experience, and any notable achievements.]
Closing	[Write a polite and professional closing, inviting the agent or publisher to request more material.]

By completing these exercises, you will gain a deeper understanding of what makes a query letter successful and how to apply these techniques to your own queries. This practice will enhance your ability to craft compelling query letters that capture the attention of literary agents and publishers.

Exercises for Identifying Your Target Audience

Exercise 1: Define Demographic Characteristics

Task: Create a demographic profile of your ideal reader. Fill in the details for each category listed below.

Goal: To understand the basic characteristics of your target audience.

Worksheet:

Demographic Category	Details
Age Range	_____
Gender	_____
Location	_____
Occupation	_____
Education Level	_____

Exercise 2: Explore Psychographic Profiles

Task: Write a detailed psychographic profile for your ideal reader. Include their interests, values, attitudes, and lifestyle.

Goal: To gain deeper insights into the interests and values of your target audience.

Worksheet:

Psychographic Category	Details
Interests	
Values and Beliefs	
Attitudes and Preferences	
Lifestyle	

Exercise 3: Analyze Reading Preferences

Task: Analyze and list the reading preferences of your target audience. Consider genre, reading frequency, and preferred formats.

Goal: To understand the reading habits and preferences of your audience.

Worksheet:

Reading Preference	Details
Favorite Genres	
Reading Frequency	
Preferred Formats (e.g., print, e-book, audiobook)	

Exercise 4: Conduct Market Research

Task: Design a survey to gather information about your potential readers' preferences, habits, and demographics. Then distribute it to your audience using tools like SurveyMonkey or Google Forms.

Goal: To collect direct data from potential readers.

Worksheet:

Survey Question	Details
Question 1	_____
Question 2	_____
Question 3	_____
Question 4	_____
Question 5	_____

Follow-Up Task: Analyze the survey results and summarize the key findings.

Exercise 5: Identify Where to Find Your Audience

Task: List online platforms and offline locations where your target audience is likely to spend their time.

Goal: To determine the best places to reach your audience.

Worksheet:

Platform/Location	Details
Online Platform 1	_____
Online Platform 2	_____

Platform/Location	Details
Offline Location 1	
Offline Location 2	

Exercise 6: Create Reader Personas

Task: Develop 2-3 detailed reader personas that represent different segments of your target audience.

Goal: To create fictional profiles that help visualize and empathize with your readers.

Worksheet:

Reader Persona 1:

Category	Details
Name	
Age	
Occupation	
Location	
Interests	
Reading Habits	
Values	
Motivations	

Reader Persona 2:

Category	Details
Name	

Category	Details
Age	_____
Occupation	_____
Location	_____
Interests	_____
Reading Habits	_____
Values	_____
Motivations	_____

Exercise 7: Engage with Your Audience Directly

Task: Plan and execute a strategy to engage directly with your audience on social media or through an email newsletter. Document the questions you will ask and the feedback you receive.

Goal: To gather firsthand insights and strengthen your connection with readers.

Worksheet:

Engagement Method	Details
Social Media Platform	_____
Questions to Ask	_____
Email Newsletter Topic	_____
Feedback Received	_____

Follow-Up Task: Summarize the feedback and discuss how it will influence your future marketing strategies.

By completing these exercises, you will gain a comprehensive understanding of your target audience, enabling you to tailor your marketing efforts more effectively and build a strong, engaged reader base.

Exercises for Building a Loyal Reader Base

Exercise 1: Consistent Communication

Task: Develop a communication plan that outlines how and when you will update your readers about your writing progress, upcoming releases, and personal milestones.

Goal: To ensure regular and consistent communication with your readers.

Worksheet:

Communication Channel	Frequency	Content Type
Newsletter	Monthly	Updates on writing progress, upcoming releases, personal milestones
Blog	Weekly	Writing tips, behind-the-scenes, personal stories
Social Media	Daily	Quick updates, photos, reader interactions
Q&A Sessions	Monthly	Live or written Q&A with readers

Exercise 2: Personal Connection

Task: Write a personal story or behind-the-scenes anecdote related to your writing journey. Share it in your next newsletter or blog post.

Goal: To create a personal connection with your readers.

Worksheet:

Personal Story/Behind-the-Scenes Anecdote:

_____
_____
_____

Platform for Sharing:

_____

Date to Share:

_____

Exercise 3: Interactive Content

Task: Create a poll or survey to gather feedback and opinions from your readers about your work or their preferences.

Goal: To engage readers and gather valuable insights.

Worksheet:

Poll/Survey Question	Response Options
What genre do you enjoy the most?	Romance, Mystery, Fantasy, Sci-Fi, Non-fiction
Which character is your favorite?	Character A, Character B, Character C
What type of bonus content would you like to see?	Bonus chapters, Behind-the-scenes, Early access

Platform for Poll/Survey:

Date to Share:

Exercise 4: Exclusive Content

Task: Plan a piece of exclusive content, such as a bonus chapter or early access to a new release, to share with your most loyal readers.

Goal: To make your readers feel special and appreciated.

Worksheet:

Exclusive Content Type	Description	Distribution Method
Bonus Chapter	A chapter revealing a character's backstory	Newsletter
Early Access	First two chapters of upcoming book	Website members-only section
Behind-the-Scenes	Photos and notes from the writing process	Social media or blog

Date to Share:

Exercise 5: Community Building

Task: Create or join an online group for your readers to discuss your books and related topics.

Goal: To foster a sense of community among your readers.

Worksheet:

Platform	Group Name	Description
Facebook	[Your Book Title] Readers Group	A place to discuss my books, share fan art, and get exclusive updates
Goodreads	[Your Name] Book Club	Monthly book discussions, Q&A sessions, and reading recommendations
Discord	[Your Name] Community	Chat with fellow readers, participate in events, and more

Date to Create/Join:

Exercise 6: Personalized Engagement

Task: Plan a personalized thank-you message to send to readers who leave reviews or share your content.

Goal: To show appreciation and build individual connections with your readers.

Worksheet:

Personalized Thank-You Message Template:

Dear [Reader's Name],

Thank you so much for your wonderful review of [Your Book Title] on [Platform]. Your support means the world to me, and I'm thrilled to hear that you enjoyed the story. If you have any suggestions or would like to share more about what you liked, I'd love to hear from you.

Best regards, [Your Name]

Platform for Sending:

Date to Send:

Exercise 7: Collaborations and Cross-Promotions

Task: Identify potential authors or influencers in your genre for collaboration. Plan a joint promotion or project.

Goal: To expand your reach and engage new audiences through collaboration.

Worksheet:

Potential Collaborator	Collaboration Idea	Benefits
Author A	Joint newsletter feature	Introduce each other's readers to new books
Influencer B	Instagram Live interview	Engage both followers with an interactive

Potential Collaborator	Collaboration Idea	Benefits
		session
Author C	Co-written short story	Combine audiences and create unique content

Date to Initiate Collaboration:

Exercise 8: Responding to Feedback

Task: Solicit feedback from your readers on a specific aspect of your work (e.g., a new character or plot twist). Plan how you will incorporate this feedback.

Goal: To improve your work and show readers that you value their input.

Worksheet:

Feedback Topic	Questions to Ask	Plan for Incorporation
New Character	What do you think of [Character Name]?	Adjust character development based on feedback
Plot Twist	Did the plot twist surprise you? Why or why not?	Enhance or clarify plot points based on responses
Book Cover	Do you find the book cover appealing?	Consider design changes based on suggestions

Platform for Soliciting Feedback:

_____

Date to Share and Gather Feedback:

_____

By completing these exercises, you can effectively build and maintain a loyal reader base that is engaged, supportive, and excited about your work. This will not only boost your book's visibility and sales but also create a strong community of readers who will eagerly anticipate your future projects.

Exercises for Content Marketing

Exercise 1: Blogging

Task: Plan and write a blog post that provides writing tips, shares a book review, or gives a behind-the-scenes look at your writing process.

Goal: To create engaging blog content that attracts and retains readers.

Worksheet:

Blog Post Topic	Writing Tips, Book Review, Behind-the-Scenes, Guest Post
Title	_____
Main Points	1. _____
	2.

Blog Post Topic	Writing Tips, Book Review, Behind-the-Scenes, Guest Post
	_____
	3. _____
	_____
Call to Action	_____
Images/Visuals Needed	_____
Publishing Date	_____

Exercise 2: Social Media

Task: Create a week's worth of social media posts, including visual content, interactive posts, and daily updates.

Goal: To maintain a consistent and engaging presence on social media.

Worksheet:

Day of the Week	Post Type	Content	Visuals Needed
Monday	Writing Tip	_____	_____
Tuesday	Book Review	_____	_____

Day of the Week	Post Type	Content	Visuals Needed
		_____	_____
		_____	_____
Wednesday	Behind-the-Scenes	_____	_____
		_____	_____
		_____	_____
Thursday	Poll/Interactive Post	_____	_____
		_____	_____
		_____	_____
Friday	Daily Update	_____	_____
		_____	_____
		_____	_____
Saturday	Live Session Announcement	_____	_____
		_____	_____
		_____	_____
Sunday	Personal Story	_____	_____
		_____	_____

Exercise 3: Email Newsletters

Task: Plan and draft your next email newsletter, ensuring it includes exclusive content, regular updates, a personal touch, and a call to action.

Goal: To keep your audience informed and engaged with consistent and valuable communication.

Worksheet:

Newsletter Section	Content
Exclusive Content	_____
Regular Updates	_____
Personal Story	_____
Call to Action	_____
Subject Line	_____
Sending Date	_____

Exercise 4: Guest Posts and Collaborations

Task: Identify potential blogs, podcasts, or authors for guest posts and collaborations. Plan a guest post or collaboration idea.

Goal: To expand your reach and engage new audiences through collaboration.

Worksheet:

Potential Collaborator	Platform (Blog/Podcast)	Collaboration Idea	Benefits
Author A	Blog	Guest post on writing strong female	Reach new readers, build credibility

Potential Collaborator	Platform (Blog/Podcast)	Collaboration Idea	Benefits
		protagonists	
Podcast B	Podcast	Interview about writing process and inspiration	Increase exposure, attract new followers
Influencer C	Social Media	Instagram Live Q&A session	Engage with mutual audiences, cross-promotion

Date to Initiate Collaboration:

Exercise 5: Video Content

Task: Plan and create a video, such as a book trailer, author interview, or writing vlog.

Goal: To engage your audience with dynamic and interactive video content.

Worksheet:

Video Type	Book Trailer, Author Interview, Writing Vlog, Tutorial
Title/Topic	

Video Type	Book Trailer, Author Interview, Writing Vlog, Tutorial
Script/Outline	1. _____ _____ 2. _____ _____ 3. _____ _____
Visuals/Props Needed	_____ _____
Platform (YouTube, Instagram, etc.)	_____ _____
Recording Date	_____
Publishing Date	_____

Exercise 6: Podcasts

Task: Plan and outline an episode for your author podcast or prepare for a guest appearance on an existing podcast.

Goal: To reach new audiences and engage listeners with valuable audio content.

Worksheet:

Podcast Type	Author Podcast Episode, Guest Appearance
Title/Topic	_____
Main Points	1. _____
	2. _____
	3. _____
Call to Action	_____
Recording Date	_____
Publishing Date	_____

Exercise 7: Content Series

Task: Plan a series of related blog posts, videos, or newsletters that cover a specific topic in depth.

Goal: To keep your audience coming back for more with serialized content.

Worksheet:

Content Series Type	Blog Series, Video Series, Newsletter Series
Series Title	
Episode 1 Title	
Episode 1 Content	
Episode 2 Title	
Episode 2 Content	
Episode 3 Title	
Episode 3 Content	
Publishing Schedule	

Exercise 8: Engagement and Interaction

Task: Plan an engagement activity, such as a fan art contest, reading marathon, or writing challenge.

Goal: To encourage participation and build excitement around your work.

Worksheet:

Engagement Activity Type	Fan Art Contest, Reading Marathon, Writing Challenge
Activity Description	_____
Rules and Guidelines	_____
Prizes/Incentives	_____
Promotion Plan	_____
Start Date	_____
End Date	_____

By completing these exercises, you can effectively utilize content marketing to attract and retain readers, establish your authority, and foster a loyal community around your work. Engaging and valuable content will keep your audience connected and eagerly anticipating your next book release.

Exercises for Building a Community Around Your Book

Exercise 1: Creating an Online Community

Task: Create and launch a social media group dedicated to your books. Plan the first month's activities to engage new members.

Goal: To establish a space where readers can connect with each other and discuss your books.

Worksheet:

Activity	Description	Date
Group Creation	Create a Facebook/LinkedIn group. Invite initial members and set group rules and guidelines.	[Start Date]
Welcome Post	Introduce yourself and the purpose of the group.	[Day 1]
Weekly Discussion	Post a discussion topic or question related to your book every Monday.	[Every Monday]
Poll	Conduct a poll about a character or plot element to gather reader opinions.	[Week 1]
Live Q&A	Host a live Q&A session to interact with group members.	[Week 2]
Member Highlight	Feature a member's post or comment to encourage participation.	[Week 3]
Contest Announcement	Announce a contest related to fan art or book reviews.	[Week 4]

Exercise 2: Engaging Through Email Newsletters

Task: Plan and draft your next three email newsletters, ensuring each contains exclusive content, updates, and reader engagement activities.

Goal: To keep your readers informed and engaged with regular, value-packed communication.

Worksheet:

Newsletter #	Content Type	Description	Sending Date

Newsletter #	Content Type	Description	Sending Date
Newsletter 1	Exclusive Content	Share a bonus chapter or deleted scene from your book.	[Date]
	Regular Updates	Update readers on your writing progress and upcoming releases.	
	Engagement Activity	Include a reader poll or survey.	
Newsletter 2	Behind-the-Scenes	Share insights into your writing process or research.	[Date]
	Regular Updates	Update readers on events or appearances.	
	Call to Action	Encourage readers to join your social media group or participate in a contest.	
Newsletter 3	Personal Story	Share a personal story or anecdote related to your book's themes.	[Date]
	Regular Updates	Announce any special offers or discounts on your books.	
	Q&A Session	Answer a few questions submitted by readers.	

Exercise 3: Hosting an Offline Book Signing

Task: Plan and organize a book signing event at a local bookstore or library.

Goal: To personally connect with readers and promote your book through direct interaction.

Worksheet:

Task	Description	Date
Venue Booking	Contact a local bookstore/library to book a venue for the event.	[Start Date]
Event Promotion	Create promotional materials (posters, social media posts) to advertise the event.	[2 Weeks Before]
Invitation	Send out invitations to your email list and social media followers.	[2 Weeks Before]
Event Preparation	Prepare a reading excerpt, signing pens, and any giveaways.	[1 Week Before]
Book Signing	Conduct the book signing, engage with attendees, and take photos for social media.	[Event Date]
Follow-Up	Send thank-you emails to attendees and share event highlights on social media.	[1 Day After]

Exercise 4: Running a Fan Art Contest

Task: Organize and run a fan art contest to engage your readers and encourage creative participation.

Goal: To foster community involvement and generate excitement around your book.

Worksheet:

Task	Description	Date
Contest Announcement	Announce the contest on your website, social media, and email newsletter.	[Start Date]
Submission Guidelines	Provide clear guidelines for submissions, including format, deadline, and criteria.	[Start Date]
Promotion	Promote the contest regularly to ensure maximum participation.	[Throughout]
Judging Panel	Assemble a panel of judges (including yourself) to review the submissions.	[Submission End Date]
Winner Announcement	Announce the winner(s) on your website, social media, and newsletter.	[Judging End Date]
Prize Distribution	Send prizes to the winner(s) and share their artwork on your platforms.	[After Winner Announcement]

Exercise 5: Partnering for a Collaborative Event

Task: Plan and execute a collaborative event with another author, such as a joint book signing or online webinar.

Goal: To reach new audiences and provide added value to your readers through collaboration.

Worksheet:

Task	Description	Date
Partner Selection	Identify and reach out to an author who writes in a similar genre.	[Start Date]
Event Planning Meeting	Schedule a meeting to plan the details of the event.	[1 Week After Start Date]
Venue/Platform Booking	Book the venue or online platform for the event.	[2 Weeks Before Event]
Event Promotion	Create joint promotional materials and share across both authors' platforms.	[2 Weeks Before Event]
Event Execution	Conduct the event, ensuring smooth collaboration and interaction with attendees.	[Event Date]
Follow-Up	Send thank-you notes to attendees and share event highlights.	[1 Day After]

Exercise 6: Developing Reader Personas

Task: Create detailed reader personas to better understand and target your audience.

Goal: To tailor your content and marketing strategies effectively by understanding your readers' needs and preferences.

Worksheet:

Persona #	Attribute	Description
Persona 1	Name	
	Age	
	Occupation	
	Location	
	Interests	
	Reading Habits	
	Values	
	Motivations	
Persona 2	Name	
	Age	
	Occupation	
	Location	
	Interests	
	Reading Habits	
	Values	
	Motivations	
Persona 3	Name	
	Age	
	Occupation	
	Location	
	Interests	

Persona #	Attribute	Description
	Reading Habits	_____
	Values	_____
	Motivations	_____

By completing these exercises, you can effectively build and sustain a vibrant community around your book. Engaging with your readers through both online and offline methods, collaborative activities, and personalized interactions will help you foster loyalty and anticipation for your future projects.

www.ingramcontent.com/pod-product-compliance
Lightning Source LLC
LaVergne TN
LVHW030321070526
838199LV00069B/6518